AMERICA the BEAUTIFUL

WISCONSIN

By R. Conrad Stein

Consultants

Howard Kanetzke, School Services Consultant, State Historical Society of Wisconsin

H. Michael Hartoonian, Ph.D., Madison, Wisconsin

Phillip Ferguson, K-6 Social Studies Chair, School District of Waukesha

Marion Rindt, Teacher, Rose Glen School, School District of Waukesha

Robert L. Hillerich, Ph.D., Bowling Green State University, Bowling Green, Ohio

CHILDRENS PRESS®

CHICAGO

Sunset on Ellison Bay, Door County

Project Editor: Joan Downing
Assistant Editor: Shari Joffe
Design Director: Margrit Fiddle
Typesetting: Graphic Connections, Inc.
Engraving: Liberty Photoengraving

FOURTH EDITION, 1992.
INCLUDES 1990 CENSUS FIGURES.

Childrens Press®, Chicago
Copyright ©1987 by Regensteiner Publishing Enterprises, Inc.
All rights reserved. Published simultaneously in Canada.
Printed in the United States of America.
    4 5 6 7 8 9 10 R 96 95 94 93 92 91

Library of Congress Cataloging-in-Publication Data

Stein, R. Conrad.
    America the beautiful, Wisconsin.

    (America the beautiful state books)
    Includes index.
    Summary: Introduces the geography, history,
government, economy, industry, culture, historic sites,
and famous people of the state which calls itself
"America's Dairyland."
    1.   Wisconsin—Juvenile literature.   [1.   Wisconsin]
I.   Title.   II.   Series.
F581.3.S84   1987   977.5   87-9376
ISBN 0-516-00495-6

Black Earth Creek meanders past a Dane County farm.

TABLE OF CONTENTS

Chapter 1

A LOOK AT WISCONSIN

A LOOK AT WISCONSIN

Picture a herd of cows grazing in a pasture. This is how most Americans think Wisconsin looks. In fact, this image is accurate. But it is not complete. Wisconsin has called itself "America's Dairyland," and is the nation's leading producer of milk, cheese, and butter. However, Wisconsin is also a major industrial state. Its factories produce everything from pots and pans for the kitchen to turbines as big as a house.

Most Americans also believe the Wisconsin countryside is a patchwork of neatly tended farms. Again, this picture is incomplete. In southern Wisconsin, a sea of farms stretches to the horizon. In the northern half of the state, forests cover most of the land. Some of the north is so untouched you could hike for many miles and meet only deer, rabbits, and an occasional black bear.

Many historians claim Wisconsin is our nation's most progressive state. "Progressive" means making use of new ideas. America's first kindergarten was established in Wisconsin. The state was first to abolish the death penalty. The system of choosing political candidates by direct primary elections originated in Wisconsin.

Wisconsin's people lead rather than follow. Its cities and its land prosper. It is an exciting state to visit and has an exciting story to tell.

Chapter 2
THE LAND

THE LAND

A Frenchman named Pierre-Esprit Radisson explored the Wisconsin wilderness in the late 1650s and wrote, "The country was so pleasant, so beautiful and fruitful . . . what labyrinth of pleasure should millions of people have [here], instead that millions complain of misery and poverty."

Radisson proved to be a prophet. In a few generations, hordes of people fled the poverty of the Old World to settle in Wisconsin. There they prospered on a generous land.

GEOGRAPHY AND TOPOGRAPHY

Wisconsin lies in the Midwest section of the United States. It is a Great Lakes state, meaning that the presence of the lakes has had a profound influence on its development. Other Great Lakes states are Minnesota, Michigan, Illinois, Indiana, and Ohio. Both Lake Superior and Lake Michigan touch Wisconsin. The Lake Michigan shoreline on the east stretches 381 miles (609 kilometers), and the Lake Superior shoreline to the north is 292 miles (467 kilometers) long. Wisconsin's territory includes several islands in both lakes.

Wisconsin's shape resembles a mitten with the thumb pointing out of the upper-right-hand corner. That slender point of land is called the Door Peninsula, though part of its northern half is actually an island. Between the Door Peninsula and the mainland

The Saint Croix River at Interstate Park, a border park established by Wisconsin and Minnesota near Saint Croix Falls

lie the waters of Green Bay. The Green Bay region played a crucial role in the state's early history.

Wisconsin is bordered by Iowa and Minnesota to the west, the Upper Peninsula of Michigan to the north, and Illinois to the south. Along the Iowa and Minnesota lines, the Mississippi and Saint Croix rivers serve as a boundary most of the way. The Menomonee, Brule, and Montreal rivers separate Wisconsin from Michigan's Upper Peninsula. Only the Wisconsin-Illinois border is entirely an imaginary line.

Wisconsin spreads over 56,154 square miles (145,439 square kilometers) of land. In size it ranks twenty-sixth among the fifty states. Its greatest distances are 320 miles (512 kilometers) north to south and 295 miles (472 kilometers) east to west. Madison is its capital city; its largest city is Milwaukee.

These farms are located in the
Western Uplands, or Driftless Area,
the only area of the state left
untouched by glacier activity.

About ten thousand years ago, an immense glacier retreated
from what is now the midwestern United States. The great wall of
ice sheared off mountaintops and filled in valleys. Today
Wisconsin has no mountains. Glacier activity left the state with
gently rolling hills that eventually became covered with forests.
Only the southwestern corner of the state was untouched by the
glacier. This fifteen-thousand-square-mile (about forty-thousand-
square-kilometer) section in the southwest is called the Western
Uplands, or Driftless Area, because no glaciers drifted over it.

The Driftless Area is strikingly different from the rest of the state. Near Camp Douglas, for example, natural sandstone towers rise like castles from a broad, flat plain, presenting scenery comparable to Colorado or New Mexico.

Wisconsin can be divided into five topographical land forms: a lowland region that runs along the shore of Lake Superior; a highland that sprawls over the northern half of the state; a central plain; a lowland area that stretches along Lake Michigan; and the western uplands that parallel the Mississippi River. Timms Hill, the highest point in Wisconsin, rises 1,952 feet (595 meters) above sea level. It stands in Price County in the heart of the Superior Uplands.

RIVERS AND LAKES

Wisconsin is a treasure trove of fresh water. People with computers who delight in totaling fantastic figures measure the state's water reserve in the thousands of billions of gallons or liters. Wisconsin has more than twenty thousand miles (thirty-two thousand kilometers) of rivers and some fifteen thousand lakes. There are so many lakes and rivers that Wisconsinites ran out of new names for them. The state has fifty-one different Beaver Creeks and seventy-four Long Lakes.

The principal rivers that flow west to empty into the Mississippi are the Saint Croix, La Crosse, Chippewa, Black, and Wisconsin. The Wisconsin, at 430 miles (688 kilometers), is the state's longest river. The Menomonee, Oconto, Wolf, Fox, Manitowoc, Sheboygan, Peshtigo, and Milwaukee rivers all flow into Lake Michigan. To the north, the Iron, Brule, Bois, and Bad rivers empty into Lake Superior. The Rock River is the only major river that flows southward into Illinois.

One of Wisconsin's nicknames is the "Land of Lakes."
Sparkling lakes nestled in deep woods delight the millions of
tourists who flock to Wisconsin each year. On a map, north-
central Wisconsin looks like a Swiss cheese because it is so dotted
with lakes and ponds. Some of these are too small to appear on
maps. Their names are known only to local people. The largest
inland lake is Lake Winnebago, which spreads over 215 square
miles (557 square kilometers). Four cities—Appleton, Neenah,
Oshkosh, and Fond du Lac—hug Lake Winnebago's shores. Lakes
Mendota and Monona help make Madison one of the loveliest
capital cities in the United States.

WILDERNESS WISCONSIN

When only Indians lived in the Great Lakes region, trees
covered much of what would become Wisconsin. Treeless prairies
were found only in the southern one-third of the state. The white
settlers who later poured into the region were the vanguard of a
growing country that demanded wood to build houses, stores, and
ships.

In a matter of decades, armies of loggers hacked down forests
that took nature centuries to grow. Devastating forest fires
ravaged those woods the loggers missed. By the end of the 1800s,
Wisconsin was a land of stumps rather than towering trees.

Today forests once again cover most of the northern half of the
state. Over two-thirds of them are owned by private companies.
Wood products such as paper, made from wood pulp, are
important to the state's economy. The paper industry brings in
about $2 billion a year. Modern Wisconsin foresters harvest trees
more carefully and scientifically than in the past. The state's
loggers now plant more trees each year than they cut down.

Lake du Bay (left) is one of approximately fifteen thousand lakes in the state sometimes called the "Land of Lakes."
Today, the forests that cover most of the northern half of Wisconsin include two huge protected areas that help preserve the state's wilderness heritage—Nicolet National Forest and Chequamegon National Forest (below).

Of the many animals that make their home in Wisconsin, deer are among the most numerous, especially in the northern forests.

Wisconsin's state tree is the sugar maple. Hardwoods make up about 70 percent of the annual timber harvest. Principal hardwoods are maple, beech, aspen, birch, oak, and hickory. Softwoods such as white and red pine, spruce, and hemlock are used to make paper pulp. Wisconsin woodlands have a delightful blend of leafy and evergreen trees. People from Illinois, Iowa, and other nearby states enjoy visiting Wisconsin's woodlands in autumn, when nature paints the leaves with a blaze of color.

Wisconsin is called the Badger State, but not because it has an overabundance of this woodland animal. The nickname came about because its early lead miners lived in dugouts, like badgers. Actually, Wisconsin could be called the Deer State. The northern forests teem with deer. Almost anyone driving the forest roads in the morning or at dusk sees at least one or two. Bears, foxes, and coyotes also live in the woodlands. Several small packs of gray wolves, now a rare animal, still roam the northern wilderness. The beaver, which was once almost driven to extinction by trappers, now thrives in rivers and ponds. Raccoons, skunks, and woodchucks are so numerous they spill into the cities and towns.

Wisconsin's lakes, rivers, and marshlands attract many species of ducks and other water birds. Grouse and pheasants live in the woods. In the lakes swim schools of bass, pike, sturgeon, and trout. The muskellunge, or muskie, is the state fish. In 1986, a man caught a fifty-six pound (about twenty-five-kilogram) muskie, the largest such fish pulled from Wisconsin waters in forty years. With specimens that big, it is no wonder that the muskie is called "the tiger of the lakes." The fisherman would not tell where he caught the fish. Like all anglers, he preferred to keep the lucky spot a secret.

The Indians relied on wild fruits and berries to supplement their diet. Forest clearings are still blanketed with plants. Ferns predominate in the north. Huckleberries, Juneberries, blueberries, and black currants grow in most parts of the state. Today Wisconsin families look upon wild-berry picking as a fun outdoor activity.

Wildflowers are the delight of spring. The lilylike shooting star blooms in all its colorful glory around Memorial Day, on bluffs overlooking the Mississippi and La Crosse rivers. The pasque flower, which resembles a tulip, sometimes blooms so early in the year it pokes its head above a blanket of snow.

Throughout the twentieth century, Wisconsinites have supported efforts to preserve their wilderness wonderland. In 1927, conservationists persuaded the state legislature to restore the eighteen-thousand-acre (seventy-two-hundred-hectare) Horicon Marsh on the Rock River in south-central Wisconsin. This vast marshland had been drained in the vain hope that crops could be grown there. When water was reintroduced, thousands of birds returned. During the 1950s, while most other states still paid only lip service to conservation, Badger State lawmakers established state forests, restricted industrial expansion in wilderness areas, and provided stiff penalties for illegal hunting and fishing. The conservation effort was led by Gaylord Nelson (who later served terms as governor and senator) and was urged on by thousands of working men and women across the state. Thanks largely to the laws passed in the 1950s and early 1960s, Wisconsin now has healthy forests and abundant wildlife.

CLIMATE

Wisconsin is a northern state and its winters are often bone-chilling. Not only are they cold, they can be frustratingly long. Milwaukee Brewers baseball games are sometimes canceled in spring because of snow, not rain. In the north, frost can coat the ground as late as July.

Summers can be as sweltering as winters are arctic. Note these extreme temperatures recorded in the state's history: the mercury reached a high of 114 degrees Fahrenheit (45.6 degrees Celsius) in July 1936, at the Wisconsin Dells, and a low of minus 54 degrees Fahrenheit (minus 48 degrees Celsius) in Danbury in January 1922. Generally, the northern part of the state is colder than the south. Milwaukee during January averages 29 degrees Fahrenheit (about minus 2 degrees Celsius) as a high and 15 degrees Fahrenheit (about minus 9 degrees Celsius) as a low. Green Bay, 114 miles (182 kilometers) farther north, has January temperatures averaging 25 degrees Fahrenheit (minus 4 degrees Celsius) as a high and 8 degrees Fahrenheit (minus 13 degrees Celsius) as a low.

Thousands of lakes and rivers attest that drought is not a problem in Wisconsin. The state receives an average of thirty inches (about seventy-six centimeters) of total precipitation (rain and melted snow) each year. In contrast, New Mexico averages

The frigid winter waters of Lake Michigan cover Door County bluffs and boulders with layers of ice.

less than twenty inches (about fifty centimeters) total precipitation each year. While drought conditions are rare, in exceptionally rainy years flash flooding can plague the state. "It was like somebody opened a bag and dumped thousands of gallons of water on us," said a Milwaukee official after a tremendous rainstorm struck the city in August 1986. The floods resulting from that storm killed two people, swamped ten thousand homes, and caused $27 million in property damage.

Chapter 3
THE PEOPLE

THE PEOPLE

Early this century, Wisconsinites demanded free college education for all qualified students, voting rights for women, minimum wages for workers, and the regulation of big business. At the time, these measures were deemed radical, but today they are laws of the entire nation. Throughout the state's history, the people have led rather than followed the nation.

WHO ARE THE WISCONSINITES?

The majority of Wisconsin residents are descendants of settlers from northern Europe. A poll taken in the 1980s reported that 51 percent of the people claimed to be at least part German. Many more listed Norway, Denmark, Sweden, and Finland as part of their heritage. German bratwurst and beer are popular items at the state's many fairs. Dozens of communities serve Norwegian *lutefisk* or Danish *kringle* at restaurants.

Despite the predominance of northern Europeans, Wisconsin enjoys great ethnic diversity. It is a "melting pot" state where people of many different backgrounds and ethnic heritages live and work side by side.

Indians were the original Wisconsinites, and today Wisconsin has a larger Native American population than any other midwestern state. Native Americans live throughout the state and work at many different jobs and professions. About 12,500 Native Americans live on eleven reservations located in the north and west. The Menominees are the state's largest Native American group. To a certain extent, reservations are "nations within a state." Inside their boundaries, Indians make and obey their own laws rather than follow state laws.

The region's first permanent European settlers were miners from the British Isles. They were followed by farmers from the eastern United States. Then came great waves of immigrant farmers from Germany, Norway, Sweden, Denmark, Finland, and The Netherlands. At the turn of the century, newcomers from Poland, Yugoslavia, Hungary, Russia, and Italy settled in the cities. They were joined by a fresh migration of Germans. Small communities of black Americans lived in the region even before statehood in 1848, but during World War I thousands of blacks came from the South to Wisconsin seeking jobs. Today, Hispanic people are among the state's newest and fastest-growing ethnic groups.

According to the 1990 census, whites make up 92.2 percent of the state's population, blacks comprise 5 percent, Hispanics 1.9 percent, and Native Americans 0.8 percent. Asians are a steadily growing ethnic group, making up 1.1 percent of the population. A sizable Hmong population from southeast Asia now lives in Wisconsin.

Religious membership is overwhelmingly Christian, divided almost equally between Catholics and Protestants. Principal Protestant groups include Lutherans, Methodists, and Presbyterians. German and Irish Catholics arrived more than a century ago, and eastern Europeans and Hispanics added greater numbers to that faith. Most of Wisconsin's Jews live in the cities. In the early 1900s, a Jewish girl named Goldie Mabovitch

Golda Meir as a young girl in Milwaukee

immigrated with her family from Russia to Milwaukee. For a few years she taught in the Milwaukee school system. Then she emigrated once more, this time to the Middle East. In 1969, as Golda Meir (the Hebrew form of her married name, Myerson) she became the prime minister of Israel.

POPULATION AND POPULATION DISTRIBUTION

The 1990 census gave Wisconsin's population total as 4,891,769. It is the sixteenth most-populous state. The 1990 population figures represent a growth of 4 percent above the state's 1980 total. The United States population during the 1980-90 period grew 9.8 percent. Like other midwestern states, Wisconsin's growth rate lags behind the population increases of the nation as a whole.

Since the 1930s, most Wisconsinites have lived in cities and towns. Wisconsin's five largest cities, ranked by population, are Milwaukee, Madison, Green Bay, Racine, and Kenosha. Milwaukee is by far the largest city, with more than three times the population of Madison. Milwaukee, Racine, and Kenosha are in the southeastern corner of the state. These three cities and their surrounding areas hold more than one-fourth of the state's total population.

Even though Wisconsin is usually thought of as a rural state, most residents live in towns or cities or their suburbs.

Far more deer than people live in northern Wisconsin. The lake port of Superior is the only large city in the northern third of the state. Some northern counties report a population density of fewer than ten people per square mile (about three people per square kilometer). The density of the state as a whole averages 90.1 people per square mile (34.8 per square kilometer). In some forested areas of the north, one can drive an hour without seeing a house or a farm.

POLITICAL WISCONSIN

Robert La Follette, a young man brimming with fresh ideas, entered the political scene in the 1880s. He believed that government should take an active role in bettering the lives of working people. He infuriated wealthy business owners and powerful old-line politicians, but average Wisconsinites revered him. His popularity began what has become a love affair between Wisconsin voters and maverick politicians. After World War II, Wisconsin voters sent Joseph McCarthy to the United States Senate. He stepped on powerful toes by claiming that Communists lurked in nearly every department of the federal government. Next, the state's voters elected William Proxmire as one of their senators. He was such an independent-minded politican that during his freshman term he publicly quarreled with the Senate majority leader and future president, Lyndon Johnson.

But Wisconsinites will not vote for a candidate simply because he or she is a rebel. Wisconsin politicians work hard to earn the respect of the voters. Above all, office-seekers must avoid scandal. In the mid-1980s, Wisconsin voters turned out of office two legislators who illegally charged the state for their personal long-distance phone calls.

For more than a hundred years, Wisconsin's voters were staunchly Republican. Many historians claim that the Republican party was born at a meeting in Ripon, Wisconsin, in 1854. Recently, however the Democratic party has become strong. In the mid-1980s, the majority in the state legislature and five of the nine congressional representatives were Democrats. William Proxmire, a Democrat, has been a United States senator for three decades. Third political parties have been important in Wisconsin, too. The Progressive party, led by Robert La Follette, was established in Wisconsin in 1924. The Socialist party was a powerful force in Milwaukee for many years.

Today, liberal politics is more at home in the cities of Madison and Milwaukee. Rural Wisconsin remains conservative. Other than that general description, it is difficult to characterize the state's politics. Wisconsin voters are fiercely independent and often defy the terms "liberal" or "conservative," or even Democrat or Republican. Wisconsinites study political issues carefully and know their candidates. Without hesitation they will vote against their customary party if they prefer the opponent. Above all, Wisconsin voters act as watchdogs over their leaders. For that reason, theirs is one of the least-corrupt state governments in the nation.

Chapter 4
THE BEGINNING

THE BEGINNING

Wisconsin is named after the Wisconsin River, which flows through the southern half of the state. The Chippewa, who are also known as the Ojibway, called this river the Weeskonsan, which is usually interpreted to mean "the gathering of waters."

THE FIRST WISCONSINITES

Archaeologists believe early human beings pushed into the Great Lakes region after the last great ice sheet retreated northwest, about ten thousand years ago. The first Wisconsinites lived primarily by hunting the herds of caribou that roamed the land. Around 7000 B.C., the climate warmed and pine and birch forests sprang up. Great Lakes people began to make jewelry, tools, and other objects from whatever material they could find. Near Green Bay, archaeologists uncovered the grave of a child who was buried thousands of years ago. Placed in its grasp was a toy whistle fashioned from the wing bone of a bird.

During ancient times, Great Lakes artisans learned how to hammer copper into axheads and spear points. Often they found copper lying in chunks on the ground. Through trial and error, they discovered how to remove raw copper from inside certain rocks. The copper culture began about 3000 B.C., and ended a few centuries later.

Among the reminders of the peoples who inhabited Wisconsin in ancient times are this Indian petroglyph rock in Jackson County (left) and a platform pyramid in Aztalan State Park near Lake Mills (above).

THE MOUND BUILDERS

In 1836, a Wisconsin farmer noticed a curious regularity about three hills on his property. The farmer wondered whether the hills could have been constructed by human beings. Upon further examination, it was discovered that the hills were actually three small, flat-topped pyramids similar to those built by ancient peoples in Mexico. The site was named Aztalan, because it was believed to be the birthplace of the fabulous Aztec culture.

The pyramids can be visited today at Aztalan State Park near Lake Mills. Archaeologists have concluded they were built about eight hundred years ago, but not by Aztecs. The creators of Aztalan were part of a culture called Middle Mississippi, which flourished in the upper Midwest from about A.D. 1100 to 1300.

The remains of at least twelve thousand mounds have been discovered in various parts of Wisconsin. Most of them were built by an even earlier group called the Effigy Mound Culture, which lived from A.D. 500 to 1100. The Effigy Mound Culture built earthen figures of birds, animals, or people. Some of Wisconsin's best-preserved effigy mounds are at Lizard Mound State Park near the city of West Bend. Featured in the park are mounds shaped like a bird, a great cat, and a lizard. Near the town of Baraboo stretches the earthen figure of a man who measures 214 feet (about 64 meters) from head to toe.

We have only vague ideas as to what forces drove the ancient peoples to build such complicated figures in the earth. The mounds' purposes seemed to vary from one era to the next. An early people called the Hopewell Culture, who lived near where the Mississippi and Wisconsin rivers meet, used mounds as burying grounds for important chiefs. The Hopewell civilization lasted from about 300 B.C. to A.D. 500. A later group called the Mississippi Culture constructed mounds as religious shrines. In some parts of the American Midwest, the Mississippi Culture lasted into the 1600s.

Though the Aztecs did not build Aztalan or the other Wisconsin mounds, contact between the Aztecs of ancient Mexico and the Mound Builders of Wisconsin might have taken place. Travel and trade routes over thousands of miles (kilometers) were common even during those times.

WISCONSIN DURING THE "CONTACT PERIOD"

In the 1630s, the region that would later become Wisconsin was thick with forests in the north. Tall-grass prairies grew in the south. The rivers flowed clear and the lakes swarmed with fish. Herds of deer roamed the forests and grasslands. Ample rainfall and rich soil gave bountiful crops to the ten to fifteen thousand people who lived within the confines of the state.

Three Indian groups predominated during the "contact period" when Indians and whites first met. The Menominees lived in the northeast along the river named for them today. Their ancestors had dwelled in the same general area for more than two thousand years. The Winnebago were spread out between the tip of Green

The Indians of Wisconsin have been harvesting wild rice in the Great Lakes area for hundreds of years.

Bay and Lake Winnebago. The Dakota lived in the northwest. Sometimes the three peoples fought brutal wars, but usually peace prevailed.

The Wisconsin Indians enjoyed a rich cultural life. An especially powerful storyteller was an honored person. Dancing to the beat of a rawhide drum was revered as recreation and as a religious experience. Passing a tobacco pipe from person to person was a cherished act of friendship. The favorite team sport was a rugged game in which a ball was advanced by players holding sticks with spoonlike scoops at their ends. The French later adopted this game and called it lacrosse.

The people of Wisconsin in 1630 grew corn, beans, squash, and tobacco. The Menominee harvested the delicious wild rice that grew on the shores of Green Bay and along inland streams and lakes. Time was told by the full moons that marked the start of the harvest season. The strawberry moon came in May and the wild rice moon in September. People lived in lodges made from saplings covered with bark. Villages were small and the groups moved with each changing season.

Wisconsin Indians believed that somewhere in the universe (but still within their grasp) existed a spirit world that was such a golden place it made the earth they lived on seem a mere shadow.

31

Individuals or groups attempted to glimpse the spirit world through endless hours of prayer or dance while denying themselves food and sleep. The chosen few who managed to see the spirit world gained special powers. Their successful journey enabled them to heal the sick and predict future events.

The Wisconsinites of 1630 traded goods with people who lived far to the east. Perhaps, although no one knows for sure, the traders spread the news that living in camps along the great river leading to the sea were strangers whose skin was as white as the winter snow. Further, they claimed that these strangers had marvelous goods, wielded powerful weapons, and preached a new religion. Probably the Wisconsinites were eager to meet these foreigners. But they had no idea that the presence of these white people meant that their old and cherished way of life would change forever.

EXPLORERS AND MISSIONARIES

Wisconsin disappointed the first white man known to have stepped upon its shores. Jean Nicolet left the French outpost at Quebec, canoed across Lake Michigan, and landed on the shore of Green Bay in 1634. He had hoped to paddle through the rivers of North America, cross the Pacific Ocean, and reach China. He even packed an elegant silk robe to impress Chinese nobles. Nicolet (and other Frenchmen) badly miscalculated the vastness of the North American continent and the Pacific Ocean. Still, the Frenchman's colorful robe dazzled the Winnebagos who greeted his canoe.

Twenty years after Nicolet's visit, French explorers Pierre Esprit, Sieur de Radisson, and Médard Chouart, Sieur des Groseilliers, made two trips to Wisconsin. Their first journey took

In 1673, during their exploration of Wisconsin, Father Jacques Marquette and Louis Jolliet crossed the Wisconsin River with their guide.

the men to Green Bay and their second to the Lake Superior shore. Radisson wrote glowing reports about the land: "Whatever a man could desire was to be had [here] in great plenty—stags, fishes in abundance, and all sorts of meat. . . ."

Black-robed Roman Catholic priests of the Jesuit order followed the explorers. The dedication of the Jesuits can be seen in the deeds of René Ménard, the first priest known to come to Wisconsin. Ménard was sick and elderly when he entered the wilderness. He lived long enough, however, to establish a mission on the banks of Lake Superior near the present-day town of Ashland.

Another Jesuit priest, Claude Jean Allouez, traveled to Wisconsin with an Indian canoeing party. The trip was perilous, and in his notebook Allouez complained, "We were forced to eat a certain moss growing upon the rocks. It is a sort of shell-shaped leaf which is always covered with caterpillars and spiders; and which, on being boiled, furnishes an insipid soup, black and viscous, that rather serves to ward off death than to impart life." Allouez survived the voyage, and in 1670 conducted a religious service on the banks of Lake Winnebago.

The region's most famous missionary priest, Jacques Marquette,

In the 1700s and 1800s, fortunes were made in the fur trade. Beaver pelts from the Great Lakes region were highly prized in Europe, where they were transformed into fashionable items of clothing such as hats (right) and coats.

was also an explorer. In 1673 he and Louis Jolliet crossed the width of Wisconsin on their way to find and explore the Mississippi River. The Wisconsin crossing required the party to paddle through the Fox River and carry their canoes overland until they reached the river the Indians called the Weeskonsan. From there the explorers pushed into country as foreign to them as the face of the moon.

As they braved the unknown, the explorers and missionaries claimed the region for the king of France. In 1672, Wisconsin became part of a huge territory called New France. Although French settlements were sparse in most of this wilderness empire, New France lasted a century and a half.

THE FUR TRADE

The Great Lakes region bore riches in the form of beaver—those remarkable animals whose fur was used in hats and coats prized in Europe. Other fur-bearing animals such as otter, fox, skunk, and muskrat lived along the many riverbanks. For two centuries, a booming fur trade was carried on between the Great Lakes and the Old World. So valuable were the animal pelts that Europeans called them "soft gold."

The fur trade had an enormous impact on the Great Lakes Indians. White people's goods—fishhooks, cotton shirts, iron pots, glass products, knives, axes, and guns—were highly prized. To obtain these items the Indians became, in effect, hired trappers for the whites. One beaver pelt traded to a white bought a small mirror. Four otter pelts could be exchanged for ten bullets to be used in a musket.

Native people fought among themselves over fur-trapping territories. In Wisconsin the Menominee, Winnebago, and Dakota peoples found themselves flooded with new neighbors who had fled wars in the east. First came the Chippewa, then the Sauk, then the Fox, the Ottawa, the Kickapoo, the Huron, and the Potawatomi. The newcomers' sudden invasion of established hunting and trapping grounds sparked many bloody battles.

One of Wisconsin's most celebrated early French settlers was Charles de Langlade. He came to Green Bay in about 1745 and established a fur-trading post on the Fox River. Born in Canada, Langlade's mother was Ottawa and his father was French. Langlade grew up with Indian people, and at an early age learned how to survive in the forests. He respected Indian traditions and spoke several Indian languages. In Wisconsin, members of his large family married their Menominee neighbors.

Although the fur trade made fortunes for a few Frenchmen, it ultimately led to the end of New France. England, which had extensive colonies along America's Atlantic Coast, wanted a greater share in the profits from furs. The two countries quarreled over boundary lines between New France and the British colonies. In 1754, war broke out in the New World and spread to Europe. In America the conflict was called the French and Indian War. The British defeated the French and their Indian allies, and a peace treaty was drawn up in 1763. The treaty gave Canada and most French possessions east of the Mississippi River to the English.

THE BRITISH PERIOD

The Indians deplored the shift in power from the French to the British. For more than a century, the French and Indians had lived side by side, and had often intermarried. The British, by contrast, were arrogant and distant in their dealings with the Indians.

In 1763, Chief Pontiac led an uprising of Great Lakes Indians against British rule. Nine British forts, including the key garrison at Mackinac, fell to the Indians. Scores of whites were slaughtered and only a last-minute rescue by Charles de Langlade saved the commander of Mackinac from execution. The Pontiac uprising was short-lived, however, because promised help from the French never arrived.

The British were soon embroiled in a war with their rebellious former colonies. The nearest land battles of the revolutionary war were fought far to the south of Wisconsin, where the American hero George Rogers Clark took three British strongholds in Illinois.

The peace treaty between the former colonies and Great Britain gave to the new United States of America all the land east of the Mississippi and south of the Great Lakes. But the Americans lacked the military muscle to wrest British soldiers from the Great Lakes forts. The British continued to control the Great Lakes and collect taxes from fur traders.

In 1818, Solomon Juneau set up a trading post at the site of what today is the busy city of Milwaukee. By 1849, Milwaukee was a bustling city of about twenty thousand people (above).

Meanwhile, permanent settlements were slowly developing in Wisconsin. Solomon Juneau and his family set up a trading post at a place the Potawatomis called Mahn-ah-waukee Seepe, which is usually interpreted to mean "council grounds." The area today is the busy city of Milwaukee. Solomon Juneau was elected its first mayor in 1846. The outpost at Green Bay grew, and the tiny villages of Sheboygan and Manitowoc appeared on the shores of Lake Michigan. Other early settlements included Fond du Lac, Oshkosh, and Appleton on Lake Winnebago; Prairie du Chien on the Mississippi River; and Portage at the crossing of the Fox and the Wisconsin rivers.

The War of 1812 drained British strength in the Great Lakes region. At the end of that war, the Americans had enough power to force British troops out of the Great Lakes forts. In Wisconsin, the United States Army built two new garrisons—Fort Howard at Green Bay and Fort Crawford at Prairie du Chien. The two forts were completed in 1816, and the Stars and Stripes now waved above Wisconsin's soil.

Chapter 5
THE PIONEER ERA

THE PIONEER ERA

My name is Yon Yonson.
I come from Visconsin.
I work in a lumber mill dar.

This song was sung in the bunkhouses of Wisconsin logging camps a century ago. The words poked fun at the accents of Swedish loggers. But Wisconsinites of the nineteenth century spoke in dozens of accents as the rich land and developing industries welcomed immigrants from various parts of the United States and nearly every country in Europe. Those nineteenth-century pioneers laid the foundations of modern Wisconsin.

THE MINING BOOM

Wisconsin's first great wave of immigrants came when lead ore, called galena, was discovered in the southwestern portion of the state. In the mid-1820s lead was valued at eighty dollars a short ton, and in one twenty-four-hour period a miner and a small crew removed eight short tons (about seven metric tons) of ore from a shaft near present-day Hazel Green. From that day forward the boom was on.

The number of miners on the southern prairies swelled from one hundred in 1825 to ten thousand in 1828. Most miners came from the southern United States, eager to try their luck in what

Tamblyn's Row, a rowhouse built of limestone blocks and logs, is part of the Pendarvis restoration in Mineral Point. Cornish miners built these and other similar houses during the lead-mining boom of the 1830s and 1840s.

was simply called "the diggins." Towns such as Platteville and Dodgeville cropped up and quickly attained the freewheeling atmosphere of California gold-rush towns. Gambling halls and saloons lined their main streets, and men walked about carrying pistols on their hips. The slightest argument was often settled with gunfire.

Mineral Point was the most brawling mining town of the era, until families from the Cornwall region of England arrived during the 1830s. The Cornish people built rows of tiny houses of limestone blocks. Some of these houses still stand and have been carefully restored. The houses were built on a hill just above the mines. According to local legend, when the women wanted to summon their men home for lunch, they stood on their front porches and waved dish towels. Consequently, the town of Mineral Point was called "Shake Rag on the Hill."

Other towns with names such as Big Red Dog, Pin Hook, and Nip and Tuck sprang up during the mining boom. Most were just a collection of shacks that vanished when the lead ore ran out. Some miners just slept inside the dugouts they burrowed, as a badger would. This practice gave Wisconsin its "Badger State" nickname. A few of the boom towns that mushroomed on the

41

prairies and then faded away were remembered in the opening
line of this poem, written by a long-forgotten resident of
Wisconsin's mining district:

> New Diggins, Shake Rag, Benton Snake
> Are all on hand and wide awake;
> Black Jack, Black Leg, Swindler's Ridge
> Claim with the rest their privilege . . .
> Beetown and Pigeon hither fly,
> With cash in hand their lot to buy;
> And last, and least inclined to nab
> Her share of mineral lands, is Grab.

THE LAST INDIAN WAR

At first the Winnebagos watched passively while white miners
invaded their land. Then, in 1827, rumors circulated that two
Winnebagos had been beaten to death while being held in jail. Led
by a warrior named Red Bird, Winnebago parties attacked a
farming settlement and killed several whites. Fearing a major
uprising, the United States Army sent five hundred cavalrymen
into the lead-mining region. Red Bird was captured, and later died
in the jail at Prairie du Chien.

The short-lived Winnebago War increased friction among
Indians and whites. The next war fought between the two peoples
remains a disgrace in the pages of American history.

The Sauk and Fox lived along the Rock River in northern
Illinois until the influx of white settlers forced them to move west.
Then one of their chiefs, Black Hawk, led a group of Sauk and Fox
back to their homeland. This action sparked the infamous Black
Hawk War fought in 1832.

The last battle of the Black Hawk War took place on the
Wisconsin side of the Mississippi River at a place called Bad Axe.

Hopelessly outnumbered, the Sauk and Fox tried to surrender. American forces stormed them, and with their backs to the river, the Indians were slaughtered. One witness later said the waters of the Mississippi were "tinged with the blood of Indians." Chief Black Hawk managed to escape but was later captured. He had started his campaign with one thousand men. After the Battle of Bad Axe only one hundred remained alive. Today, people of Wisconsin consider Chief Black Hawk a hero and a military genius.

The defeat spelled doom for many of Wisconsin's Indians. Winnebago Chief Little Elk lamented his people's plight when he spoke at Prairie du Chien: "The first white man we knew was a Frenchman. . . . He smoked his pipe with us, sang and danced with us, married some of our women, but he wanted to buy no land. The 'Redcoat' came next. . . . But [he] never asked us to sell our country to him! Next came the 'Bluecoat' [the American] and no sooner had he seen a small portion of our country, than he wished us to sell it ALL to him. . . . Why do you wish to add our small country to yours, already so large?"

STATEHOOD

The United States Congress had lumped Wisconsin together with what would become Michigan, Illinois, Indiana, Ohio, and parts of Minnesota and the Dakotas to form what was called the Northwest Territory. This huge region was created when Congress passed the Northwest Ordinance in 1787. The ordinance established procedures that eventually made the Northwest Territory part of the new United States. Following an orderly plan, sections of the Northwest Territory became individual territories. Then, when the individual territory reached a

The Northwest Ordinance, passed by the United States Congress in 1787, created the Northwest Territory, which included what are today the states of Wisconsin, Michigan, Illinois, Indiana, Ohio, and parts of Minnesota and the Dakotas.

population of sixty thousand non-Indian settlers, it was eligible to become a new state. One of the most far-reaching acts ever passed by Congress, the Northwest Ordinance served as a model for the admission of new states and promoted the growth of the country from sea to sea.

The Wisconsin Territory was established on July 3, 1836. Its boundaries included present-day Wisconsin, Iowa, Minnesota, and part of the Dakotas. The first territorial legislature met in a frame building near the town of Belmont in the fall of 1836. Henry Dodge, a rugged pioneer who had fought in the Black Hawk War, served as the first territorial governor. Dodge was a leading citizen in the rough-and-tumble lead-mining region. His primary political opponent was James Doty from New York. Doty had been born into a well-to-do family, and came west hoping to make a fortune by buying and selling land.

After a stormy first session, the territorial legislature chose a lovely but empty woodland to be the site of the capital. They called the spot Madison in honor of the United States president, James Madison. But this choice was stained with scandal. James Doty had purchased 1,300 acres (520 hectares) of land at Madison only a few months earlier. He reaped enormous profits by selling back parcels of land to the state and to private investors.

Congress whittled away Wisconsin's borders before granting statehood to the territory. First, Congress moved its southern border sixty miles (ninety-six kilometers) north to give Illinois access to Lake Michigan ports. Without this change, the city of Chicago would be in Wisconsin. Then Wisconsin's northernmost region was given to Michigan, and is now that state's Upper Peninsula. Finally, Congress determined that the Mississippi and Saint Croix rivers would form most of Wisconsin's western and northwestern borders.

In the spring of 1846, the people of the Wisconsin Territory approved the move toward statehood by a five-to-one vote. On May 29, 1848, President James K. Polk signed the act that made Wisconsin the thirtieth state to be admitted to the American Union. Nelson Dewey was the state's first governor.

THE YANKEES

When the Erie Canal connected the Hudson River with Lake Erie in 1825, travel to the Midwest became immensely easier. Farmers from the East, mainly from New York State and the New England states, began to emigrate to Wisconsin. These people, who were usually called Yankees, brought farming experience, established ideas of township government, and a respect for education. Often they built school buildings before town halls.

The Yankees and other immigrants settled the southern half of

The construction and improvement of Racine's harbor between 1844 and 1873 was a major factor in the growth of the industrial town.

the state first. There they found rich grassy plains ripe for growing crops. They had grown wheat in the East, so they planted it here. Though it was a challenge to cut through the thick mat of roots left by prairie plants, wheat became the state's primary crop. Nearly all farm families kept one or two milk cows, however. As Wisconsin grew during this time, no one guessed how important dairy products would become to the state.

Pioneer areas usually attract religious leaders determined to create utopias in the wilderness. Wisconsin was no exception. James Jesse Strang claimed that God came to him in a dream and said, "[You] shall plant a stake of Zion in Wisconsin. . . ." In the early 1840s, Strang and his followers operated a religious community in western Racine County. Strang ruled as if he were a medieval king, and anyone disobeying his wishes was tied to the whipping post and lashed. A gentler religious community was founded at Ripon. Called the Ceresco Colony, its members were not allowed to own personal goods. Instead, they devoted themselves to communal living and religious study.

Then as now, the population concentrated in the southeastern corner of the state. Milwaukee developed from two villages, Juneautown and Kilbourntown, that merged in 1839. Milwaukee's population stood at 21,000 in 1850, but leaped to 46,000 the very next year. A few miles south, Kenosha's population grew from 337 in 1842 to more than 1,000 twelve months later. Nearby Racine enjoyed similar growth.

THE EUROPEANS ARRIVE

"An endlessly fresh spirit surges through this land. Wherever you direct your gaze, something great can be seen developing." These words begin a letter written in 1854 by Carl Schurz, whose passionate fight against slavery made him one of the most honored Americans of his time.

By the end of the 1850s, more than one third of the state's population was foreign-born. Half that group were Germans. Some of the Germans, Carl Schurz among them, were highly cultured, educated men and women who escaped a bloody revolution that swept their land in 1848. But the majority of German immigrants were simply farmers who wanted to till Wisconsin's rich soil. They looked to the intellectuals for leadership. In Milwaukee, Germans who fled the revolution were called "forty-eighters." They established theaters and built concert halls in the city. In Watertown, Margarethe Schurz, wife of Carl Schurz, founded the first kindergarten in America in 1856.

Irish immigrants were second in number to the Germans. Swiss people settled in Green County where they made Swiss cheese in the city of Monroe. Danes gathered along the Lake Michigan shore and spread from Racine north to the tip of the Door Peninsula. Racine boasted that it was the "most Danish city in America." Finns, Norwegians, and Swedes spread throughout the state.

HOW THE SETTLERS LIVED

Early farm villages were made up mostly of people from the same ethnic background. Norwegian was the common language spoken in Norwegian villages, German in German villages, and so on. Ethnic differences were seen even in village buildings. For example, most Finnish households had an additional room or a tiny house for a sauna bath. Nevertheless, many people worked away from their home village. A German might run a flour mill in a Norwegian village or a Yankee own a general store serving a Finnish town.

Using sweat, muscle, and ingenuity, farm families built houses and fed themselves with little more than what the raw land gave them. Houses were made from logs with plaster daubed between them. Only when a family prospered were the log huts replaced with frame houses. Potatoes were a staple food, and most farmers hunted and fished to bring some variety to the table. Pioneer women had the never-ending and lonely jobs of milking, cooking, scrubbing pots and pans, tending to the garden, and sewing by candlelight long after the other family members had gone to bed.

Winter was the pioneers' worst enemy. Naturalist and writer John Muir, who grew up on the Wisconsin frontier about a hundred years ago, wrote: "The only fire for the whole house was the tiny kitchen stove . . . around which in hard-zero weather all the family of ten persons shivered, and beneath which in the morning we found our socks and coarse, soggy boots frozen solid. . . . We had to squeeze our throbbing, aching, chilblained feet into them, causing greater pain than a toothache."

Still, the rich soil of Wisconsin was productive. Writing her grandmother from a farm near Fond du Lac, a frontier girl named Clara Chaney proudly described her accomplishments: "We have

The Republican party, formed primarily to fight slavery, held some of its earliest meetings in Ripon in 1854 (above). Political activist and slavery foe Carl Schurz, shown here in a political cartoon of the times (right), campaigned for the 1860 election of his close friend, Republican presidential candidate Abraham Lincoln.

got all our garden planted. It contains potatoes, beans, peas, summer and winter squash, beets, pumpkins, watermelons, carrots, cucumbers, onions, and lettuce and cabbage. And a nice lot of tomatoes and a little Indian corn which is good to eat green. I have a small flowerbed, but I mean to have a first-rate one next year."

THE CIVIL WAR

The European settlers, especially the German intellectuals, eagerly joined the crusade against slavery. In Milwaukee a mob once stormed the jailhouse to free a runaway slave being held there for his southern master. The Republican party, which was formed primarily to fight slavery, held some of its earliest meetings in the town of Ripon in 1854. Slavery foe Carl Schurz was a close friend of Republican presidential candidate Abraham

This Civil War Memorial in Milwaukee honors the eighty-five thousand Wisconsin soldiers who fought for the Union.

Lincoln, and traveled the country making speeches on his behalf. When Lincoln was elected president, Schurz wrote a friend how pleased he was that he had "contributed something toward raising the breeze which carried Lincoln into the presidential chair and thereby shook slavery to its foundations."

When the bloody Civil War erupted in 1861, Wisconsin contributed eighty-five thousand soldiers to the Union Army. Some twelve thousand of them died, costing the state more lives lost than in any war since. Wisconsin soldiers fought so bravely that General William Tecumseh Sherman, commander of Union forces in Georgia, once said, "We estimated a Wisconsin regiment equal to an ordinary brigade." The most honored of the state's war heroes was an eighteen-year-old Milwaukeean named Arthur McArthur who won the Congressional Medal of Honor by leading a charge up a Confederate-held hill. His son Douglas (who changed the spelling of his family name to MacArthur) was one of the country's highest-ranking generals in World War II.

The Rhinelander Logging Museum—a reproduction of a nineteenth-century logging camp—brings to life the era's most important industry. On the grounds are several pieces of logging equipment, including a steam hauler and a narrow-gauge logging engine.

CHANGING THE FACE OF THE LAND

Until the mid-nineteenth century, the northern two-thirds of Wisconsin was covered with some of the most splendid forests in North America. In the Chippewa River Valley alone stood one-sixth of the nation's white pine trees. No one believed that the lush Wisconsin woods could ever be completely chopped down. But an army of loggers—directed by wealthy timber barons and helped by the railroads then being built—reduced the magnificent forests to fields of stumps in less than one lifetime.

The lumber companies worked from south to north. After they cleared the forests, they sold the land in parcels to farmers who pulled the stumps and planted crops. People had believed that forestland was unsuitable for farming. But except for the far north, crops grew well in fields that once nourished trees. As the logging industry marched relentlessly northward, the blanket of trees was replaced by a patchwork of farms.

A Milwaukee newspaper claimed: "Wheat is king, and Wisconsin is the center of the empire." At the time, Wisconsin was the nation's second-largest wheat-producing state, and Milwaukee was its busiest wheat-shipping port. Then a stubborn insect called the chinchbug ravaged Wisconsin's wheat fields. Also, farmers in the new states to the west—Kansas, Nebraska, and the Dakotas—found their land even more suited to wheat

When the Peshtigo fire of 1871 broke out on the afternoon of October 8, townspeople fled toward the river to escape the roaring wall of flame that engulfed the town.

growing than was Wisconsin's soil. Clearly, the state's farmers needed something new.

In 1864, an entrepreneur named Chester Hazen opened one of the state's first cheese factories. Rival business people predicted it would go bankrupt, but six years later fifty other cheese-processing plants were operating in the state. Experienced Swiss, Dutch, and German cheesemakers showed the way. A crusading newspaper editor named William Dempster Hoard, who later became governor, urged wheat farmers to shift to milk production. Hazen, Hoard, and others founded the Wisconsin Dairymen's Association in 1872. The University of Wisconsin aided the dairy revolution when Professor Stephen M. Babcock invented a method for testing the butterfat content in milk. Soon pastureland and herds of cows had replaced wheat fields, and Wisconsin became "America's Dairyland."

The most dramatic and deadly change in the land occurred at a forested area north of Green Bay. In 1871, the town of Peshtigo was a lively lumbering port ringed by an immense forest. On the afternoon of October 8, an eerie yellow light appeared in the sky and white ashes fell upon the town like snow. On the main street someone yelled, "Fire!" A raging forest fire surrounded Peshtigo. No one is sure how the conflagration started. Sweeping faster than a man can run, walls of flame pressed into the town's streets. Families bolted from their houses and raced toward the river. Horribly, some people burst into flame while on the run. Those who reached the river stood in neck-deep water as the raging wall of fire consumed their town. A survivor who watched the hellish scene from the river wrote, "I saw nothing but flames; houses, trees, and the air itself were on fire."

The inferno swept north toward the Michigan border. Unbelievably, a second fire started on the opposite side of Green Bay. On that awful night, twelve hundred people were killed, almost twice that many were injured, and 1,280,000 acres (512,000 hectares) of forestland were destroyed. The Peshtigo Fire was one of the nation's gravest disasters. Yet no national newspaper carried the story until long after the flames had died out. The reason was that the Great Chicago Fire broke out that same night and dominated America's headlines. Consequently, only local papers reported the Peshtigo tragedy. One of their writers penned this poem:

> Cities in ashes, towns swept out of sight,
> Millions on millions destroyed in one night!
> The eighth of October, for long years ahead,
> Remembered by many that longed for their dead.

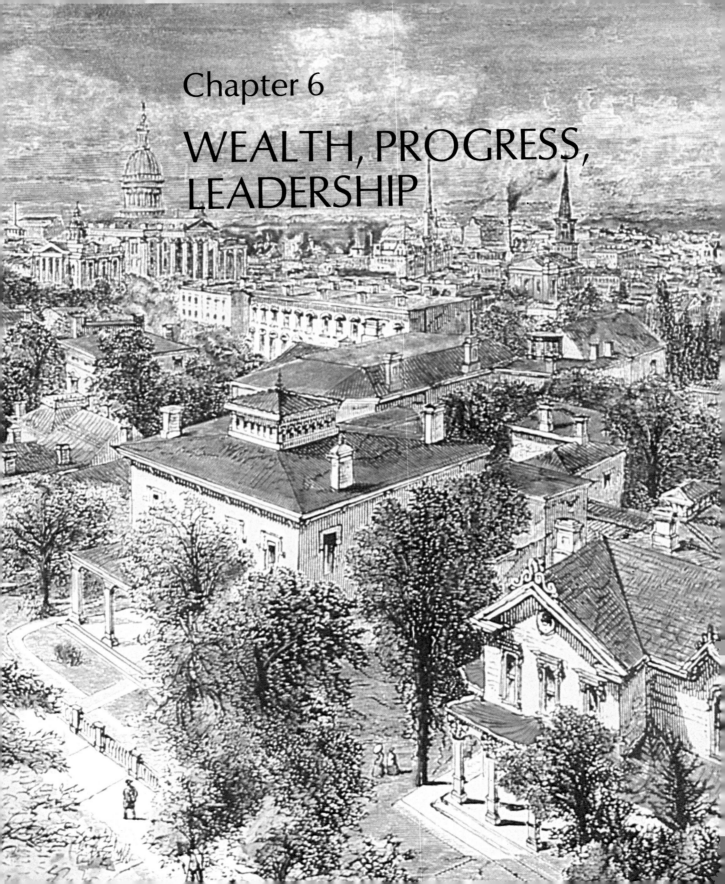

Chapter 6
WEALTH, PROGRESS, LEADERSHIP

WEALTH, PROGRESS, LEADERSHIP

The cure for the ills of democracy is more democracy.
—Senator Robert M. La Follette
McCarthyism is Americanism with its sleeves rolled.
—From a speech praising Senator Joseph P. McCarthy
Why do so many of our officials decide to spend the taxpayers' money in ways that are patently futile and for no general good?
—Senator William Proxmire

THE DEVELOPMENT OF INDUSTRY

Owners of huge lumber companies were Wisconsin's first industrial giants. In the late nineteenth century, their powers extended into state government. Cadwallader C. Washburn owned vast pinelands and a sawmill at La Crosse. Washburn served in the state assembly and was elected governor in 1872. Harrison Ludington, a Milwaukee merchant and another "pine millionaire," became governor in 1876. The state's most powerful political boss of the times was lumber baron Philetus Sawyer, whose empire was headquartered in Oshkosh.

In contrast to the pine millionaires, the lumberjacks were woefully underpaid. But they gave the state rich memories. The "jacks" were a gambling, fighting, drinking group of restless souls who sang songs and told tall tales when they weren't beating each other up. On Saturday nights the jacks turned logging towns such as Ashland, Rhinelander, La Crosse, Eau Claire, and Hurley into shambles with their shenanigans. During the week, they worked in freezing weather and slept in bunkhouses so Spartan that there weren't even facilities for taking a bath. It was said that a logger who once bathed in a downtown hotel told a fellow worker that baths were very healthy. "I agree," said the other jack. "I took a bath last year and I ain't been sick since."

Railroads sprang up to carry the lumber to market. The largest of all Wisconsin railroad companies was the Chicago, Milwaukee and St. Paul, owned by the tough but brilliant Alexander Mitchell. At Mitchell's death in 1887, his railroad company was one of the nation's richest lines. Though many people hailed the railroad's contributions to the growth of the state, farmers cursed the high freight rates they had to pay to ship their crops to city markets.

The Great Chicago Fire of 1871 destroyed most of that city's breweries. So Milwaukee beer makers such as Best, Miller, Schlitz, and Pabst sent their beer to the people of Illinois. Beer drinkers there enjoyed Milwaukee beer because it was brewed using traditional German methods. By 1872, half of Milwaukee's beer was being sold to out-of-town buyers. Milwaukee became the "beer capital" of the nation—a title it has held ever since.

The two decades from 1880 to 1900 saw the number of factories in Wisconsin double and the number of workers increase threefold. A thriving paper-products industry developed in Green Bay and in cities along the Fox River. Milwaukee became a leading producer of leather products, boots, and shoes. Steam shovels made in the Milwaukee area helped to dig the Panama Canal. Factories producing metal goods in Kenosha, Racine, and Beloit expanded.

Wisconsin's industrial revolution drew hordes of people to the

The Blatz Brewery in Milwaukee as it looked in 1879, when Milwaukee
had already earned the title "beer capital of the nation."

state. In 1860, the state's population stood at 775,881; in 1870, it
was 1,054,670; in 1880, 1,315,497; in 1890, 1,693,330; and in 1900,
2,069,042. As in the past, many of the newcomers came from
Europe. A huge second wave of Germans migrated to Wisconsin
during the 1880s, and in Milwaukee two out of three people
preferred German-language newspapers to those printed in
English. Thousands of immigrants from Poland and Italy also
arrived. Most of the newcomers sought work in the industrial
cities.

ROBERT MARION LA FOLLETTE

Wisconsin's rapid industrialization came with a price tag. By
1900, railroad, logging, and industrial tycoons controlled state
government as if it were their own private club. Anyone wishing
to run for public office had to have the support of these Old-guard
men, most of whom were members of the Republican party. Then
a Republican lawer named Robert Marion La Follette entered the
state's political picture.

When this 1905 photo was taken on Nicolet Street in Madison, Robert M. La Follette—whose Progressive Republicans had succeeded in making sweeping changes in the state laws—was ending his term as governor and beginning his first term as a United States senator.

Born near Madison, La Follette grew up on Wisconsin's log-cabin frontier. He attended the University of Wisconsin, and while there heard a speech by Edward G. Ryan, chief justice of the Wisconsin Supreme Court. La Follette often quoted Ryan's words, which lingered in his mind for the rest of his life: "For the first time really in our politics money is taking the field as an organized power. . . . The question will arise which shall rule, wealth or man; which shall lead, money or intellect; who shall fill public stations, educated and patriotic free men, or the feudal serfs of corporate capital?"

La Follette married Belle Case, a brilliant young woman from Baraboo. She was the first woman graduate of the University of Wisconsin Law School. Belle La Follette was a fighter for women's voting rights, an antiwar crusader, and a leading advocate of giving full rights to black people. La Follette once said of his wife, "Her grasp of the great problems, sociological and economic, is unsurpassed by any of the strong men who have been associated with me in my work."

One day La Follette was called to the Milwaukee hotel room of Philetus Sawyer, who was a lumber baron, a political boss, and a United States senator. The senator offered the young lawyer a handsome fee if he would help in a pending case soon to be tried by a circuit judge who happened to be La Follette's brother-in-law. According to La Follette's autobiography, he shouted in reply, "Senator Sawyer, you can't know what you are saying to me. If you struck me in the face you could not insult me as you insult me now."

La Follette's fight with Senator Sawyer split Wisconsin's Republican party into an old-guard wing and a new group called the Progressive Republicans. From it La Follette also gained his nickname, "Fighting Bob." Running under the Progressive banner, La Follette was elected governor in 1900. He was the first Wisconsin governor born in the state.

THE PROGRESSIVE ERA

La Follette and the Progressive Republicans made sweeping changes in Madison. Laws were passed to regulate the freight rates charged by the railroads. A state civil-service law was enacted, and the groundwork was laid for the passage of a graduated income tax.

The Progressive Republicans' major political victory over the conservatives was the enactment of a new nominating process to screen candidates for elective offices. Previously, party bosses met and chose most candidates. In 1904, the Progressives opened up the nominating process by enacting the Direct Primary Law. Under the new law, people wishing to run for office first entered a primary election held by each political party a few months before the general election. Through primaries, the voters—not the politicians—decided which candidate would represent each party on the election ballot. Wisconsin was the first state to have direct primary elections, and the principle was soon adopted by other states.

In Milwaukee, voters turned to the Socialist party because it backed an eight-hour day for workers, and because the city's previous administration was so corrupt. The Socialist movement was also strong in Germany, and attracted many immigrant voters. In 1910, the Socialist party reached the peak of its strength in Milwaukee, when it elected a mayor and won control of the city council. The power of Milwaukee's Socialists soon waned, and they never again matched their 1910 success. But in 1914, Socialist Dan Hoan won the mayor's job and held it until 1940.

La Follette went to Washington as a senator in 1906. He remained a senator for almost twenty years. In Washington, he advocated strict railroad regulation, the expansion of national parks, and laws prohibiting child labor. One of his major victories was the passage of a law that improved the working conditions for merchant seamen.

Some Republicans hoped La Follette would be nominated for president, but their dreams were dashed by World War I. La Follette was passionately opposed to America joining the war that raged in Europe. "War is always cruel," he wrote. "Its iron tread means destruction and devastation. . . ." Critics questioned his patriotism. A Chicago newspaper charged, "La Follette is acting as a German because there is a large German vote in Wisconsin."

La Follette broke with the Republican party in 1924, and ran for president at the head of a new political organization called the Progressive party. He received almost five million votes—the

The three members of the La Follette family political dynasty shown here are Senator Robert M. La Follette, Sr., (top left, without hat); Senator Robert Marion, Jr. (above); and Governor Philip F. (left).

highest up to that time for a third-party candidate—but he carried only Wisconsin.

Robert La Follette died the year after his presidential bid, but he left Wisconsin a political dynasty that remains active today. His wife became an important member of the Woman's Committee for World Disarmament. One son, Robert Marion, Jr., was elected senator immediately after his father's death and served for more than twenty years. A second son, Philip, served two terms as governor in the 1930s. In the 1980s, Bronson C. La Follette, Fighting Bob's grandson, was the state's attorney general.

HARD TIMES AND WAR

The 1920s saw the last great influx of Europeans to Wisconsin. Unlike previous eras, most of these immigrants came from southern and eastern countries in the Old World. By 1920, Poles were the second-largest ethnic group in the state. On Milwaukee's South Side one heard more Polish than English. Italians settled in Milwaukee, Kenosha, and Madison. Other Europeans arrived from Yugoslavia, Czechoslovakia, Hungary, and Greece.

Wisconsin's black population remained small compared to that of neighboring Michigan and Illinois. Before World War I, fewer than 3,000 blacks lived in Wisconsin. The 1930 census recorded 10,739 black citizens. More than three-quarters of Wisconsin's blacks lived in Milwaukee.

The arrival of blacks, European Catholics, and Jews upset some Wisconsinites. In 1921, a Madison newspaper carried this advertisement: "Wanted: Fraternal Organizers, men of ability between the ages of 25 and 40. Must be 100% Americans." The ad was sponsored by the Wisconsin branch of the Ku Klux Klan (KKK), which was anti-black, anti-foreign, anti-Catholic, and anti-Jewish. By 1924, the Wisconsin branch of the KKK claimed a membership of seventy-five thousand. But three years later, the Klan was almost nonexistent in the state. While the Klan's activities captured many headlines, the overwhelming majority of Wisconsinites were hostile to the white-robed group. When KKK members tried to hold a parade through downtown Mazomanie, the citizens there pelted them with eggs.

In 1921, Coach Earl ("Curly") Lambeau brought his obscure football team into the newly formed National Football League. During their first season, the Green Bay Packers won ten games while losing only one. It was the beginning of a love affair

Since 1921, the Green Bay Packers have been Wisconsin's football team.

between the people of Wisconsin and the football team from Green Bay. Today the team is owned by the Green Bay community, and plays some of its games in Milwaukee's County Stadium.

The decade of the 1920s ended with the stock-market crash that left the nation in the grips of the Great Depression. The once-humming factories in Milwaukee, Green Bay, Superior, Racine, Kenosha, Stevens Point, and Janesville ground to a halt. As the depression worsened, farmers saw the prices they received for milk dip so low they could hardly afford to feed their cows. Striking farmers poured their milk on the ground rather than sell it at prices that would lead to bankruptcy.

Under Governor Philip La Follette, the Wisconsin legislature acted to ease the crisis. The state began a $7 million program that was designed both to improve roads and create jobs. In 1932, the legislature enacted an unemployment-insurance law that gave money to jobless people. It was the first such law passed anywhere in the country, and served as a model for a similar law later enacted by the federal government.

During the World War II years, Wisconsin's 383,000 workers produced $12 billion worth of material, including trucks, guns, ships, machine tools, mess kits, infantry boots, and blankets. The state's farms produced more than half the nation's cheese and one-third of its evaporated milk. Wisconsin became the country's leading producer of vegetables for canning.

About 300,000 Wisconsin men and women served in the armed forces during World War II. The state's most important soldier was Milwaukee-born Douglas MacArthur, Commanding General of the United States Army Forces in the Far East. Richard Bong, a fighter pilot from Poplar, shot down forty Japanese aircraft and was one of seventeen Wisconsin natives to win the Congressional Medal of Honor. Carl Zeidler, the mayor of Milwaukee, took leave of his job to join the navy just after the Japanese bombed Pearl Harbor. Zeidler was killed when his ship went down in 1942. He was one of 7,980 Wisconsinites who failed to return when the bells of peace finally chimed over the land in 1945.

THE POSTWAR YEARS

As a political party, the Progressive movement died in 1946 when Robert M. La Follette, Jr. was defeated in the Republican primary election for senator. For the first time in more than forty years, no La Follette family member held prominent office in Wisconsin. Replacing La Follette was a man from Appleton named Joseph R. McCarthy.

Senator McCarthy won national fame on the basis of one

COMMUNIST PARTY ORGANIZATION U.S.A.-FEB. 9, 1950

Senator Joseph McCarthy (with pointer) during the infamous 1954
Army-McCarthy hearings

issue—his personal crusade against communism. In 1950, he
charged that the State Department was dominated by Communist
party members. Though investigations held by a Senate committee
found no Communists in the State Department, McCarthy
continued hurling accusations. His tough talk won him admirers
among the American people. A new term—"McCarthyism"—
entered the political vocabulary. It was used to describe politicians
who gained power by accusing their enemies of being
"Communist sympathizers."

Wisconsin's voters reelected Joseph McCarthy to the Senate in
1952, but by a slim margin. He later fought off a recall effort
whose motto was "Joe Must Go!" In 1954, McCarthy made his
boldest move when he accused the United States Army of
"coddling Communists." During a nationally televised
investigation, many Americans grew to dislike McCarthy's
boorish and bullying tactics. He failed to prove Communists had
infiltrated the army, and after the investigations he was censured
by the Senate. In 1957 McCarthy died, a broken and bitter man.

For Wisconsinites, one of the most joyous events of the 1950s was the Boston Braves baseball team's move to Milwaukee. The move meant that the world of baseball finally regarded Milwaukee as a major-league city. As was true with the Green Bay Packers, all of Wisconsin fell in love with the Braves. Players such as Henry Aaron and Eddie Mathews became larger-than-life heroes. Schoolchildren singing "The Star-Spangled Banner" ended the song with the words: "O'er the land of the free and the home of the *Braves*."

The state's economy shifted direction in the 1950s and 1960s as manufacturing became more important than agriculture. Although production of milk and milk products remained high, the number of dairy farms dropped. Migrant farm workers, many of whom came from Mexico, sought jobs in the cities. Milwaukee's now-sizable Mexican community developed during this period.

Throughout the 1960s, Democratic governors such as Gaylord Nelson and John Reynolds battled Republican-dominated legislatures. The drawing of Congressional districts was among the hottest issues. In 1962, Wisconsin voters sent Gaylord Nelson to the United States Senate, where he became an influential member and a leading environmentalist. Bidding for his fourth term as senator, Nelson was defeated in 1980 by Republican Robert W. Kasten, Jr., who was reelected in 1986.

MODERN WISCONSIN

By the late 1960s, Milwaukee was one of the most segregated large cities in the country. Blacks were confined to a tiny belt of streets often called the "inner core." Whites in nearby neighborhoods spread the message that they would not tolerate a black family living next door. In 1967, Milwaukee's blacks began a

When he violated a ban on demonstrations by joining the 1967 fair-housing protest in Milwaukee, civil-rights activist Father James E. Groppi (center, with glasses) was arrested.

campaign urging the city's Common Council to pass a fair-housing ordinance. Within the council, the effort was directed by Milwaukee's only black council member, Vel Phillips. On the streets she was joined by white clergyman James Groppi, who led bands of chanting black protesters into white neighborhoods on the city's South Side. Fistfights broke out and rocks and bottles were thrown. Tempers eased somewhat when the Milwaukee Common Council passed an open-housing ordinance in 1968.

On a September morning in 1970, a Madison police telephone operator received this message: "Okay, pigs, now listen and listen good. There's a bomb in the Army Math Research Center—the University—set to go off in five minutes. . . ." Less than two minutes later, before the police could issue a warning, an explosion rocked the University of Wisconsin campus. A

During the 1980s, not all Wisconsin farms were as prosperous as this one. When crop prices dropped and bank loans became impossible to repay, many farms were auctioned off to the highest bidder.

researcher working inside the Math Center was killed and four others were injured.

The tragic bombing occurred amid the gloom of the Vietnam War, and the radicals who had planted the explosives claimed they did so because the math department was involved in research for the United States Army. The bombing capped months of unrest on the University of Wisconsin campus. During the 1960s and early 1970s, Madison was one of the most politically active campuses in the nation. After the explosion, years passed before a sense of calm returned to the university.

In 1978, Governor Patrick J. Lucey left office after six years and was appointed by President Jimmy Carter to be ambassador to Mexico. Although he knew very little about the problems of that country, he became a popular American representative.

In Washington, Senator William Proxmire campaigned against wasteful government spending. In 1976, he began his monthly "Golden Fleece Award," designed to draw attention to outlandish and expensive projects funded by the federal government. Proxmire awarded one "Fleece" to a tax-supported study that hoped to discover why monkeys, rats, and humans clench their teeth. "Did that question ever bother you?" asked Proxmire. "Bother you enough to feel that our government should spend $500,000 to find some kind of answer?"

Mirroring the rest of the Midwest, Wisconsin farmers were plagued by debts in the 1980s. A decade earlier, the federal government had encouraged farmers to borrow in order to expand their operations. Because farm prices were rising steadily, expansion seemed to be a good idea. But then crop prices dropped, leaving farmers saddled with enormous debts and reduced means to pay back their bank loans. Many a farmer had no choice but to allow the bank to take over the farm and auction it off to the highest bidder. Across the state, farmers wept as they saw their land, which might have been in their family for a hundred years, sold to strangers.

Early in the 1980s, Wisconsin suffered through the pangs of the business recession that gripped the country. Kenosha, the home of several automobile-producing plants, was particularly hard hit. Then, in 1986, the Chrysler Corporation agreed to manufacture luxury cars in Kenosha, and it seemed as if the city would bounce back from its troubles. But two years later, Chrysler changed its mind and announced it would halt car production in the city. Chrysler's move cost Kenosha at least 5,500 jobs. At the auto plant a sign went up saying KENOSHA HAS BEEN CHEATED.

In 1986, Wisconsinites chose Republican Tommy Thompson to be their governor. During the campaign, Thompson promised to cut government spending and hold taxes in line. After his victory, Thompson declared, "The people elected me to cut state spending, and that's what I'm going to do."

With problems on the farms and in the cities, Wisconsinites look to the 1990s with mixed emotions. But, as always, they are a confident and positive people.

Chapter 7

GOVERNMENT AND THE ECONOMY

GOVERNMENT AND THE ECONOMY

Today a state can prosper only with an efficient government and a thriving economy. Wisconsin enjoys harmony between the state government and the private business sector. The government provides services that private industry does not perform, and private businesses employ the vast majority of Wisconsin's workers.

STATE GOVERNMENT

Wisconsin's constitution serves as its legal foundation. The constitution was ratified March 13, 1848, just before President James K. Polk signed the bill making Wisconsin the thirtieth state. It has been amended more than 125 times, but has never been rewritten. This makes it the sixth-oldest constitution of all the states. The place in which it was written, a home called Hazelwood in Green Bay, is now a museum.

The constitution patterns the Wisconsin government after the federal government of the United States. State government has three main divisions, or branches: the executive; the legislative; and the judicial. The executive branch is responsible for enforcing laws, the legislative branch makes new laws and rescinds old ones, and the judicial branch interprets laws.

The executive branch is headed by the governor and the lieutenant governor. They are elected together to four-year terms.

The constitution permits the governor to appoint heads of agencies and state commissions. As the person responsible for enforcing laws, the governor may send the state militia to any troubled area. The governor may also free a person held in a Wisconsin jail. Other important constitutional officers in the executive department are the secretary of state, the treasurer, the attorney general, and the state superintendent of public instruction.

The Wisconsin legislature consists of two houses: a thirty-three-member senate and a ninety-nine-member assembly. Senators are elected to four-year terms and representatives to two-year terms in the assembly. The legislature decides whether proposals, called bills, should become laws of the state. In 1981, for example, the Wisconsin legislature discussed 2,009 bills and voted to enact only 385 of them into laws. Before a bill can become a law it must be signed by the governor. On occasion, the governor may veto, or refuse to sign, a bill. When that happens, the legislature, with a two-thirds vote, can enact the bill into law even without the governor's approval.

Working with the governor, the legislature prepares the state's budget. About half of Wisconsin's tax money comes from workers who pay an income tax and from businesses that pay a corporation tax. A sales tax levied on purchased goods is another important source of revenue. Wisconsin also receives grants from the federal government. Taxes on gasoline and license fees for cars and trucks help maintain roads. Fees collected for hunting and fishing permits aid state conservation programs.

Wisconsin's judicial branch consists of a seven-member supreme court, a twelve-member court of appeals, sixty-nine circuit courts, and more than two hundred municipal courts. All state judges are elected on nonpartisan ballots. This means a

These students at Milwaukee's Hawley Road School are among Wisconsin's more than 525,000 elementary-school students.

candidate for the office of judge need not declare a political party. Supreme court judges are elected for ten-year terms. The supreme court is the state's highest judicial body.

Locally, Wisconsin is divided into 72 counties that embrace 187 cities, 393 villages, and 1,267 towns. County government is particularly important in farm areas where political and even social life centers on the county courthouse. Each county is governed by a board of supervisors elected by the voters.

EDUCATION

A state government pamphlet issued in 1986 boasted that "On national tests, Wisconsin elementary and secondary school students consistently score much higher than the national average and higher than the average of other midwestern states." Another state publication says that "Wisconsin ranks first in the U.S. in ACT [American College Testing Program] scores of high school seniors."

The public school system was established in Wisconsin in the 1850s. Today the state has more than 525,000 elementary and

Bascom Hall (right), is the centerpiece of the University of Wisconsin's Madison campus. Privately operated Mount Mary College (above) is in Milwaukee.

275,000 secondary students. They are served by 431 school districts. Running this vast system is expensive. In 1985 it cost the state $3,237 to educate each student.

More than 157,000 Wisconsin elementary and secondary students attend private schools. Most private schools are church-affiliated. The Roman Catholic Diocese of Milwaukee operates one of Wisconsin's largest private school systems.

The state has thirty-two privately operated colleges and universities. Carroll College in Waukesha, Beloit College in Beloit, Ripon College in Ripon, and Lawrence University in Appleton are the oldest and most respected of the smaller private institutions. The largest private university, Marquette University in Milwaukee, serves thousands of urban students, and in recent years has gained fame for its strong basketball teams.

Public higher education is served by the University of Wisconsin system. In 1971 the University of Wisconsin at Madison merged with various state universities to create a system of twelve branch campuses and fourteen two-year institutions that now serve 160,000 students. The branches are at Eau Claire,

Green Bay, La Crosse, Milwaukee, Oshkosh, Kenosha (Parkside), Platteville, River Falls, Stevens Point, Menomonie (Stout), Superior, and Whitewater.

Founded in 1848, the University of Wisconsin at Madison is one of the finest schools in the world. In the 1890s, the university gained its reputation for liberalism. The slogan of the school, in the spirit of Robert La Follette's progressive "Wisconsin Idea," was taken from a board of regents report in 1894:

> Whatever may be the limitations which trammel
> inquiry elsewhere, we believe that the great state
> University of Wisconsin should ever encourage that
> continual and fearless sifting and winnowing by
> which alone the truth can be found.

Today the University of Wisconsin is a center of medical and scientific research. Nearly eighteen thousand people work there. Biotechnology is an important field of study. Working with farmers and businesses, University of Wisconsin scientists have produced improved seeds and new methods of treating illnesses.

The Madison campus also has a rare beauty rivaled by few other university sites. From classrooms and dormitories, professors and students can gaze upon sparkling Lake Mendota.

MANUFACTURING

Wisconsin is most famous as "America's Dairyland." But manufacturing is really its largest single enterprise. Since World War II, Wisconsin has ranked eleventh among the fifty states in industrial production and twelfth in factory employment. Each year more than eight thousand factories turn out more than $22 billion worth of goods. Almost five hundred thousand workers earn their living in manufacturing.

Canned cherries and aged cheese are among the products made by Wisconsin's food-processing industry, the second-largest industry in the state.

Nonelectric machinery is a $5-billion-a-year business. This includes machine tools such as drills and lathes, power cranes, farm machines, and construction equipment.

Food processing is the state's second-largest industry. Some two hundred kinds of cheese are made in the state, including colby, Wisconsin's own creation. Wisconsin remains a leading brewer of beer. Most breweries are located in Milwaukee, but the fast-growing G. Heileman Company is headquartered at La Crosse. One of every four cans of sweet corn sold in the United States comes from Wisconsin. Other foods that roll out of the state's canning plants include canned beets, peas, lima beans, cherries, and sauerkraut.

Endowed with vast forests, Wisconsin leads the country in the manufacture of paper products. Major paper mills are in Green Bay and along the Fox River. The gigantic Kimberly-Clark mill in Neenah produces millions of rolls of bath tissue. All told, Wisconsin provides 12 percent of the nation's paper products.

Other important industries include autos and trucks, leather goods, metal products, household appliances, wood products, and rubber and plastic items. Kenosha, Janesville, and the Milwaukee area are auto-making centers. Milwaukee leads the leather-tanning industry. Factories in Manitowoc produce metal products of various kinds. The town of Kohler, near Sheboygan, is a principal maker of plumbing fixtures.

AGRICULTURE

Wisconsin will surely remain America's Dairyland through the 1990s. The state's two million dairy cows produce almost three billion gallons of milk each year. Nearly three-fourths of this milk is made into cheese. Milk and milk products account for $3 billion in yearly sales. No other state approaches Wisconsin in dairy production.

Wisconsin has ninety-four thousand farms, which average about 198 acres (about 79 hectares) in size. The richest farms are concentrated in the south, where farmers can count on a longer growing season. Wisconsin farmers lead the nation in hay production and are among the leaders in green peas, beets, cabbage, sweet corn, and cranberries. Eggs from poultry farms are an important product.

In the north, the growing season is only a hundred days long, which discourages delicate crops. Hogs and beef cattle thrive there. Turkeys and ducks are raised throughout the state.

NATURAL RESOURCES

Wisconsin's first big population boom came because of lead mining in the 1820s. Today mining plays only a small role in the state's economy. Sand and gravel, zinc, and dolomite are mined in various places. Iron ore is mined in Jackson County in the west-central section of the state. Wisconsin is second in the United

States after Arkansas in diamond production, but the number of gems mined remains small.

The forests covering the northern half of the state contribute to the lumber, pulp, plywood, and paper-products industries. More than two-thirds of all Wisconsin forestland is privately owned. Commercial fishing is carried on from waterfront towns on the Lake Michigan and Lake Superior shores, but fishing is no longer a major enterprise.

Wisconsin's greatest natural gifts are rich soil, plenty of water, and the kind of wild beauty and recreational space that attracts tourists.

TRANSPORTATION AND COMMUNICATIONS

Wisconsin has about 5,000 miles (about 8,000 kilometers) of railroads and 108,000 miles (172,800 kilometers) of paved highways. In 1917, Wisconsin became the first state to identify its highways by number, and other states soon followed its lead.

Fifty harbors provide entry from Lake Huron, Lake Superior, and the Mississippi River. Oceangoing ships traveling the Saint

The harbor at Superior is a major port for iron ore from Minnesota.

Lawrence Seaway stop at the Lake Michigan ports of Kenosha, Racine, Milwaukee, Manitowoc, and Green Bay. The city of Superior shares the western end of Lake Superior with Duluth, Minnesota, and is a major port for iron ore from Minnesota. River barges haul cargo to western Wisconsin towns along the Mississippi River.

Wisconsin has more than four hundred airports, the busiest of which is Mitchell Field in Milwaukee. The private carrier Air Wisconsin serves more than thirty-three cities in Wisconsin and neighboring states.

About 325 newspapers are published across the state. The largest of the dailies are the *Milwaukee Journal*, the *Milwaukee Sentinel*, the *Green Bay Gazette*, and the *Wisconsin State Journal* of Madison. Over the years, the *Milwaukee Journal* has won many awards for its outstanding reporting.

Wisconsin has 225 radio stations and 22 television stations. Public broadcasting is provided by the University of Wisconsin, the State Educational Communications Board, and other educational agencies and nonprofit organizations. Eight television and 30 radio stations provide public broadcasting throughout the Badger State.

Chapter 8
ARTS AND LEISURE

ARTS AND LEISURE

Wisconsin prospers largely because its people relish hard work. But Wisconsinites also enjoy the arts, sports, and the outdoor life that nature placed on their front steps.

LITERARY WISCONSIN

Wisconsin's literary tradition began just after the Civil War with poet Ella Wheeler Wilcox. Born in Dane County in 1850, she wrote a complete novel before reaching the age of ten. Wilcox was a spiritualist who claimed to be able to communicate with her dead husband. She called herself a "poet of passion," and these lines confirmed her view:

> Sometimes I feel so passionate a yearning
> For spiritual perfection here below,
> This vigorous frame with healthful burning,
> Seems my determined foe.

George W. Peck was an important figure in the state's literary and political history. He served as Wisconsin's governor from 1891 to 1895, and as a sideline wrote books for young readers. His "Peck's Bad Boy" series of comic novels had children rolling with laughter. Peck defied the tradition of the times, which presented child characters as little angels. His boy hero was a mischievous but lovable brat.

Ella Wheeler Wilcox (left), was Wisconsin's first literary figure. George W. Peck wrote a series of comic novels whose hero was a mischievous but lovable brat (above).

At the start of this century, Hamlin Garland was revered as the dean of Wisconsin writers. His works recount the rugged life of the Wisconsin frontier, and his book *A Daughter of the Middle Border* won the Pulitzer Prize in 1922. Also in the 1920s, novelist Glenway Wescott probed the problems of a young man growing up in an isolated Wisconsin town. In 1928 he wrote a bitter book, *Good-bye Wisconsin,* and moved to Europe.

Many modern Wisconsin-born writers such as Thornton Wilder and sports reporter Walter Wellesley "Red" Smith abandoned their state to live in more heralded literary centers such as Chicago and New York City. Red Smith won a coveted Pulitzer Prize for his sportswriting in 1976. Another Pulitzer Prizewinner was John Toland, a native of La Crosse. Other well-known Wisconsin writers are Zona Gale, Edna Ferber, Laura Ingalls Wilder, Marguerite Henry, and Maureen Daly.

In the 1980s, the trend of native-born writers moving out of Wisconsin shows signs of reversing. Chicago-born writers such as Norbert Blei have moved to Door County, north of Green Bay.

The north-central town of Rhinelander is home to the Rhinelander School of Arts, which every summer features a writers' workshop.

The little-known but now highly respected poet Lorine Niedecker lived her entire life on the shores of Lake Koshkonong, which lies just north of Janesville. She died in 1970 after a long career writing for small poetry magazines. Eventually, Niedecker's lines caught the favorable eye of critics. One of her short poems is called "Santayana's":

> For heaven's sake, dear Cory,
> I don't know poetry?
> I like somewhat the putrid Petrarch
> And the miserable Milton
> I don't have books
> Don't meet important persons
> Only an occasional stray student
> Or an old Boston lady.

THE FINE ARTS

Hidden in downtown Milwaukee are scores of architectural surprises, some more than a century old. The Mitchell Building and the Mackie Building, both constructed in the 1870s, stand side by side, looking like two Victorian wedding cakes. The buildings are a celebration of curlicues and granite gingerbread. The nearby Federal Building, completed in 1892, is a Milwaukee landmark. The triangular-shaped Milwaukee City Hall with its clock tower 350 feet (105 meters) tall has dominated the city skyline since 1895. Many of Milwaukee's older buildings were built with distinctive cream-colored granite blocks and bricks, giving rise to one of Milwaukee's nicknames, the "Cream City."

Some examples of Milwaukee's modern architecture are the

Among Wisconsin's architectural surprises are the Milwaukee City Hall with its tall clock tower (above) and Taliesin, Frank Lloyd Wright's beautiful home and studio in Spring Green (left).

Center for the Performing Arts, a downtown theater complex built in 1968 and 1969, and the First Wisconsin Center, a towering office building completed in 1974.

The present State Capitol building, which has risen over the center of Madison since 1909, is one of the most impressive capitols in the United States. Its base is in the form of a Greek cross, and its massive dome rests on the four wings.

Wisconsin-born Frank Lloyd Wright, who died in 1959, is often hailed as America's foremost architect. Although he is known primarily for his works in Chicago, many of Wright's most imaginative buildings stand in his native state. A magnificent house called Taliesin served as Wright's home and studio at Spring Green. Its lines follow the contours of the hill upon which it is perched. Perhaps the most famous of Wright's Wisconsin structures is the S.C. Johnson & Sons office building and research tower in Racine. The magazine *Architectural Record* said of the Johnson Wax complex, "These buildings shine in uncompromising purity and deliver all that the spirit may wish."

Milwaukee's Pabst Theater, built in 1895 and renovated in 1986, presents a variety of entertainment including concerts, musicals, drama, and dance.

Wisconsin has produced many famous painters and sculptors. Helen Farnsworth Mears (1876-1916) was a brilliant sculptor whom critics called "the genius of Wisconsin." Georgia O'Keeffe was born at Sun Prairie in 1887, and during an incredibly long career became one of America's most celebrated modern artists. Her paintings of flowers and desert scenes are highly personal and feature unique splashes of color. She died in 1986.

The state has many museums, including the Wright Art Center at Beloit, the Paine Art Center in Oshkosh, the Milwaukee Art Center, and the new State Historical Museum on Capitol Square in Madison. The Wisconsin Rural Art Group exhibits paintings and works of sculpture created by the state's farmers.

Milwaukee has an outstanding symphony orchestra and a ballet company that began as a small club in the 1970s. "This is really an arts community," said Ted Kivitt, director of the Milwaukee

Ballet. "They want quality and they support it. I've never seen so many people work so hard to keep something going."

Folk music is popular in the university community of Madison. During the warm months, it is common to see folk groups or a lone singer performing on the sidewalks. Throughout the state are groups devoted to preserving the songs and native dances of Germany, Poland, Norway, Sweden, Mexico, Italy, and a score of other cultures.

Carrie Jacobs-Bond, a native of Janesville, wrote many sentimental songs that stirred the souls of music lovers early in this century. Two of her most popular songs are "I Love You Truly" and "The End of a Perfect Day."

Milwaukee hosts more than a dozen legitimate theaters. The Pabst Theater has served the city since 1895. In Madison, theater companies perform nearly every night of the year. Drama lovers travel from as far as England to attend the summer sessions of the American Players Theater at Spring Green. The company specializes in the works of Shakespeare.

FAIRS AND FUN

For farm people nothing equals the excitement of the Wisconsin State Fair, which claims to be "the state's oldest and largest annual event." The first fair took place in 1851, and eighteen thousand people attended. More than nine hundred thousand people have gone to the State Fair during each year of the 1980s. Typically, the fair features high-school bands, livestock-judging contests, and a host of carnival rides. But Wisconsinites have had a long tradition of adding spice to the event. In 1902, fair officials staged a spectacular head-on collision between two railroad locomotives, each thundering down the track at sixty miles

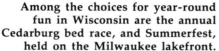

Among the choices for year-round fun in Wisconsin are the annual Cedarburg bed race, and Summerfest, held on the Milwaukee lakefront.

(ninety-six kilometers) per hour. In 1986 they held a pig race on Nothing Could Be Swiner Day.

Milwaukee's street fairs, presented by different ethnic groups, are an explosion of music, dancing, and delightful food. Guests at the Irish Fest meet a leprechaun and dance a country jig. *Piñatas* are shattered to the wild beat of mariachi music during Fiesta Mexicana. The Afro Fest is billed as "a family celebration with African food, music, arts, and crafts." Festa Italiana is one of the largest Italian festivals celebrated in the nation.

Scores of communities hold festivals celebrating a locally made product or an aspect of town history or culture. Monroe celebrates its Cheese Days Festival in September. Featured events are Swiss dances, a children's parade, and instructions on how to make Swiss cheese. Madison, the intellectual center of Wisconsin, hosts an arts fair called the Festival of the Lakes. The Madison Symphony Orchestra plays while ballet dancers perform on the streets. The Lumberjack World Championships are held in Hayward, and contestants compete in chopping, tree-climbing, and log-rolling contests.

Circus wagons on display at the Circus World Museum in Baraboo

But not all fairs or tournaments have to celebrate something serious. The national Watermelon Seed Spitting Championship is decided each year in Pardeeville. The farmers of Sauk City stage an unusual tournament every Labor Day weekend—the annual Cow Chip Throwing Contest.

The famous Ringling Brothers Circus was founded in Baraboo in 1884. The Circus World Museum in Baraboo displays a fantastic collection of equipment used by early circus companies. Around 1900, a teenager from Appleton joined the circus as a trapeze artist. He later turned to magic, and under the name Harry Houdini, thrilled the world with his seemingly impossible escape acts. In 1985, Milwaukee revived a long-standing tradition by holding an old-fashioned circus parade, complete with caged animals and acrobats.

Food is part of the fun of Wisconsin. Legend claims that the Door County Fish Boil was invented by the region's lumberjacks. It is a stew made from fish, potatoes, and onions, all cooked in the same pot. The Cornish pasty—a pastry turnover filled with meat and potatoes—was brought to Wisconsin by miners from

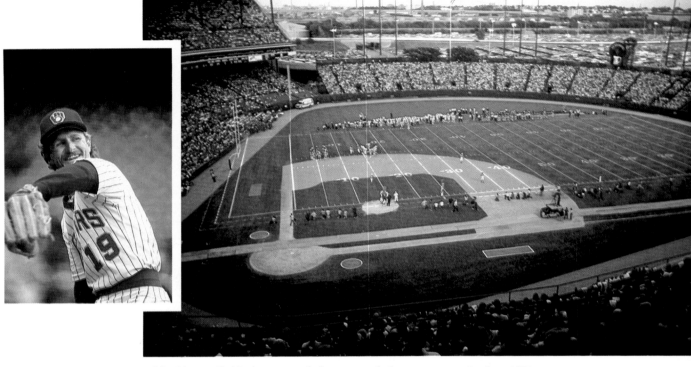

Robin Yount (left) was one of the stars of the pennant-winning 1982 Milwaukee Brewers, who play in Milwaukee County Stadium (above).

Cornwall in Britain. The tasty meat pie is sold at stands in dozens of towns. Most of all, Wisconsin is famous for its spicy German sausages called bratwursts. They are served in a bun like a hot dog and are often smothered with grilled onions or sauerkraut. Vendors sell ''brats'' from stands at Milwaukee's County Stadium, from pushcarts that rest in the shadow of the State Capitol's dome, and in the most remote North Woods towns.

SPORTS

The beloved Milwaukee Braves, who had come from Boston in 1959, moved to Atlanta in the 1966 season, leaving thousands of frustrated baseball fans behind. Then, in 1972, a new club called the Brewers opened in Milwaukee. A decade later, under manager Harvey Kuenn, the Brewers won an American League pennant. Stars of that team included Gorman Thomas and Robin Yount.

The Milwaukee Bucks, the city's professional basketball team, was a fledgling organization until 1969 when towering center Lew Alcindor joined the club. He changed his name to Kareem Abdul-Jabbar and led the Bucks to a championship in 1971. Abdul-Jabbar was traded to Los Angeles, but the Bucks remained a strong team. Under popular coach Don Nelson, stars such as Sidney Moncrief and Terry Cummings have kept the Bucks contenders in the mid-1980s.

Football fans' passionate loyalty to the Green Bay Packers was nurtured during the 1960s, when coach Vince Lombardi molded perhaps the most powerful team in football history. Lombardi's winning philosophy was simple: "I demand a commitment to excellence and victory—and that is what life is all about." Lombardi and players such as Bart Starr, Ray Nitschke, Willie Davis, Forrest Greg, and Herb Adderley won league titles in 1961, 1962, and 1965, and were victorious in the first two Super Bowl games in 1966 and 1967.

But after the Lombardi era, Packer fans began to ask the sad question, "What have you done for us lately?" Aside from a strong showing in 1972, the Packers fielded mediocre and dismal teams through the mid-1980s. Nevertheless, at the start of every new season Wisconsinites proclaim, "The Pack is back!"

In 1986, the magazine *Sports Illustrated* devoted an issue to amateur sports in the Appleton area. In this city of about 58,000 people, it reported, 270 softball teams suit up each summer week. The magazine concluded, "The ethos of Appleton is: Work hard, play hard. So when the sun sets here, the games on softball fields and basketball courts are just beginning."

Throughout the state during the summer there is competition in volleyball, track and field events, and a host of water sports. In winter, popular sports include skiing, curling, tobogganing,

Wisconsin is the setting for an amazing variety of outdoor activities, from rock climbing in Devil's Lake State Park (above) to canoeing on the Oconto River (right).

skating, sledding, and hockey. And leave it to Wisconsinites to dream up sporting contests in fields where no one else dares to tread. Madison holds an annual boat race that requires all vessels to be built from empty milk cartons. Nearly a hundred milk-carton boats competed in the 1986 event.

OUTDOORS WISCONSIN

Whether they are factory workers in Kenosha or college professors in Madison, all Wisconsinites are just steps away from the exciting world of nature. Wisconsin has forty-nine state parks, nine state forests, twenty-nine canoe routes, and thousands of miles of hiking trails and bike paths.

With endless lakes and streams, Wisconsin is a paradise for fishing enthusiasts. The premier game fish is the muskellunge, or muskie, a hard-muscled battler known for its graceful leaps out of the water. The northern pike is the second-largest and second-most important game fish. The record northern hooked in Wisconsin waters weighed thirty-eight pounds (about seventeen kilograms).

Hunting is strictly controlled in Wisconsin because state officials wish to preserve the wildlife herds. But there are no restrictions on snapping pictures of wild animals. Spend a day in the Wisconsin wilderness and you will almost certainly be able to photograph a white-tailed deer or two. A lucky photographer might even snap a soaring eagle, a bobcat, or a timber wolf.

Rock hunting is a popular activity along the state's lonely miles of lakeshore. Sharp-eyed beachcombers can spot moonstone, quartz, agate, and a wide variety of fossils. Bluffs along the Mississippi also hide mineral treasures. Even diamonds have been discovered in Wisconsin near Oregon, Waukesha, and Plum City. More diamonds probably remain in the soil today, waiting to be found by a lucky rock hound.

Hikers and backpackers enjoy trekking the state's countless miles of trails. The most challenging is the Ice Age Trail. It stretches more than a thousand miles (sixteen hundred kilometers) through breathtaking scenery. Laid out in 1971, the Ice Age Trail follows the edge of debris left when the last glacier retreated from the region.

While visiting Wisconsin, it is only necessary to keep the senses open. As a state tourist department pamphlet says, "Go to a north country lake and hear the cry of the loon. Visit Horicon Marsh and feel the rush of wind as a thousand Canada geese take flight. Find a comfortable seat under a tree overlooking a pond and watch a beaver build a dam. There are sights and sounds that you will experience in the Wisconsin outdoors that will stay with you all your life."

Chapter 9

HIGHLIGHTS OF THE BADGER STATE

HIGHLIGHTS OF THE BADGER STATE

In northern Illinois and Indiana, bumper stickers urge "Escape to Wisconsin." Indeed, the many attractions of the Badger State make it a delightful escape for tourists. Wisconsin has wild rivers, jewel-like lakes, lush forests, busy cities, quiet towns, and a fascinating assortment of museums and historical centers. In order to cover just a sampling of Wisconsin highlights, probably the best plan is to start in the south and work north.

THE SOUTH

All along the Illinois-Wisconsin border, billboards advertise stores that sell cheese. Specialty cheese stores are found throughout the state, but they are concentrated here. The stores offer a delightful variety of cheeses, most of which are made in Wisconsin.

Kenosha and Racine rank among the state's largest cities. Kenosha is a large automotive center where several plants conduct walking tours to allow visitors to see how cars are assembled. Another Kenosha highlight is the beautiful lakefront campus of Carthage College located on the northern edge of town. Racine boasts the Racine County Historical Museum, the Racine Zoo with its fine collection of birds, and the S.C. Johnson & Son headquarters building, designed by famed architect Frank Lloyd Wright.

At Old World Wisconsin, nineteenth-century German, Norwegian, Finnish, and Danish farms, as well as a crossroads village of the 1870s, have been restored to look as they did during the pioneer era.

For generations, the Lake Geneva area has been a playground for wealthy families. Elegant homes line the lakeshore, and the area has a unique mail system. Mail is delivered from a slow-moving boat by a mail carrier chosen for "athletic ability." The carrier hops off the bow of the boat, stuffs the letters into a mailbox, and then jumps onto the stern. If the mail carrier is a step too slow, a dunking will surely occur.

Old World Wisconsin lies at the town of Eagle, near Milwaukee. Sprawling over 576 acres (about 230 hectares), the site features farmsteads and villages typical of Wisconsin's past. Men and women dressed in clothing styles of an earlier time demonstrate daily activities such as soap making, rug weaving, and the harvesting of hay. This living museum opened its gates in 1976. Its farmhouses, barns, churches, and stores, which number more than forty buildings in all, were moved from various parts of the state and carefully restored to look as they did during the pioneer era. It takes more than a full day to see all of Old World Wisconsin, but a visit of any length provides a wealth of pleasant memories.

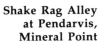

**Shake Rag Alley
at Pendarvis,
Mineral Point**

Wisconsin history comes to life in other southern towns. At Mineral Point, visitors can see Pendarvis, a group of restored stone houses built by miners in the 1830s and 1840s. The Mining Museum at Platteville features a walk into a lead mine first opened in 1845. Stonefield Village rises near Cassville along the Mississippi River. It was named for the farm owned by Wisconsin's first governor, Nelson Dewey. The village was built to look like a typical farming town at the turn of the twentieth century. Wisconsin's Agricultural History Museum is also located in Stonefield. The Villa Louis Mansion at Prairie du Chien is now a historic site. Villa Louis once belonged to the family of fur trader Hercules Dousman, who made a fortune trading beaver pelts and in railroading.

The Wisconsin River once served as a lifeline for the fur trade. Today it is a scenic waterway, paralleled by a road that leads into the quiet towns of Bridgeport, Boscobel, Blue River, and Muscoda. River bluffs close to Wauzeka contain the Kickapoo Caverns. This labyrinth of caves has existed since the Ice Age, and sometimes was used as a home by the Kickapoo Indians. Near Prairie du Sac is Natural Bridge State Park. Here a natural bridge, fashioned by wind erosion, forms a graceful arc over the forest floor.

Milwaukee's
Mitchell Park
Conservatory

MILWAUKEE AND MADISON

Frequent travelers often comment that Milwaukee is the friendliest city in the land. People there take the time to chat and share their city with visitors. It is an exceptionally clean town that boasts a county-wide park system spreading over 14,500 acres (5,800 hectares). In fact, it is sometimes called the "City of Parks." A ride on a Lake Michigan cruise boat is an entertaining way to see Milwaukee's skyline. The newest pleasure craft, the *Star of Milwaukee*, takes tourists to the Milwaukee harbor, its river, and the lovely lakefront parks. The handsome Pabst Theater building, built in 1895 and founded by the brewery family, stands in the heart of downtown. At Twentieth Street and Wisconsin Avenue, visitors can tour the imposing Pabst Mansion, built in 1893.

At the Milwaukee County Zoo the large animals stare at visitors from across moats, not through the bars of cages. Three huge glass domes at the Mitchell Park Conservatory house its vast collection of plants, flowers, and shrubs. Milwaukee offers visitors four art museums and seven museums that concentrate on human history, natural history, and applied science. If touring museums makes you hungry, you will find everything from Middle Eastern

Madison, the capital, lies on a narrow isthmus of land between Lake Mendota and Lake Monona.

shishkebab to Japanese sushi in Milwaukee. The city's ethnic restaurants serve German, Chinese, Czechoslovakian, Italian, Mexican, Polish, Greek, and southern food delicacies.

Madison is one of the prettiest smaller cities in America. It is centered on a narrow isthmus that separates Lake Monona from Lake Mendota. Other lakes lie within the city limits or nearby. Parks are laced along the shores of these lakes, and the residents enjoy swimming, boating, and fishing.

In the heart of Madison rises the Wisconsin State Capitol, whose dome towers almost as high as the Capitol in Washington. Made of gleaming white granite, the building is bathed in floodlights at night and can be seen for miles. The University of Wisconsin campus is just a short walk from the Capitol. On Madison's East Side stands the handsome governor's mansion.

A must during a trip to Madison is a visit to the State Historical Society Museum. Exhibits there tell the story of the Badger State. Displays are designed to spark children's imagination. Newly completed glass-enclosed exhibits depict the way Indian peoples lived in Wisconsin long before the Europeans arrived.

CENTRAL WISCONSIN

The central part of the state is a pleasant blend of towns, farms, and wilderness areas. In many small towns, children who gaze out of their classroom windows see cows grazing in pastures. Productive and picturesque, central Wisconsin can be thought of as the state's heartland.

North and west of Milwaukee is the rolling Kettle Moraine country. This land was sculpted by the glacier that inched over it ten thousand years ago. Holy Hill at Hubertus affords a spectacular view of the Kettle Moraine State Forest. Nearby Lizard Mound State Park contains effigy mounds built by Indian people in prehistoric times. Visitors driving to the two wilderness areas often stop at the city of West Bend to hunt for bargains at the many factory outlet stores that sell clothes and shoes. The Kettle Moraine Scenic Drive (county highway T) has its terminus at Elkhart Lake. This small town is also the home of Road America, the oldest and longest automobile racing track in the nation. The lakefront village of Port Washington attracts sport-fishing fans who hope to land a Lake Michigan trout or a coho or chinook salmon.

Farther north along Lake Michigan's shores are the towns of Sheboygan, Manitowoc, Two Rivers, and Kewaunee. Bratwurst lovers claim that the very best "brats" are made in Sheboygan. Near Sheboygan stands the Old Wade House, built in 1851 as an inn to house weary stagecoach travelers and now a historic site. Here visitors see more than a hundred restored carriages displayed at the Jung Carriage Museum. For generations, Two Rivers was a headquarters for commercial fishing. Though fishing is no longer a major industry, hardy trawlers still ply the waters and people come from miles around to buy the "morning catch."

Mustang fighter planes line up at the Oshkosh Experimental Aircraft Association Fly-in

In Manitowoc, visitors board the U.S.S. *Cobia*, one of twenty-eight submarines that were built in the town's shipyards during World War II. The exhibit of wooden clipper ships at the Manitowoc Maritime Museum is the only such exhibit in the country.

Farther north is Green Bay, Wisconsin's oldest settlement, the state's third-largest city, and the home of the Green Bay Packers football team. Want to buy season tickets to the Packer games? You'll have to join a waiting list of twenty thousand names. The Green Bay Packer Hall of Fame stands on Lombardi Avenue across from Lambeau Field. It is a museum chock full of Packer memorabilia, including the shoes of one player who wore a size 15EE.

To the south, the cities of Appleton, Neenah, Oshkosh, and Fond du Lac cling to the shores of Lake Winnebago. Oshkosh has won worldwide fame for its annual Fly-in. Each July, thousands of experimental and antique planes congregate at the Oshkosh airport. The planes displayed include vintage fighters from World War I and II. "You could spend days here and not see everything. It's fabulous," said a Swiss visitor to the 1986 convention.

Beyond Winnebago, the towns of Wausau, Marshfield, Stevens Point, and Wisconsin Rapids lie tucked between farmland and wilderness areas. Stevens Point relies mainly on manufacturing, but residents enjoy easy access to rivers, lakes, and forestland. Wausau is a diverse small city that has more than 150 factories and stores and is a center for the insurance industry. Rib Mountain and Council Grounds State Parks are popular playgrounds for local people.

Wisconsin has ten thousand miles (sixteen thousand kilometers) of charted bicycle trails. Perhaps the finest one connects the heartland towns of Elroy and Sparta. The paved pathway is built above an abandoned railroad bed and over bridges and through tunnels. Totaling about thirty-three miles (about fifty-three kilometers), the Elroy-Sparta bike trail carries a rider on a pleasant journey past woods and quiet farms.

One of the state's most widely visited regions is the Wisconsin Dells, about a seven-mile stretch (about eleven kilometers) of fantastic canyons and gorges carved out by the tireless Wisconsin River. Indian lore claimed that the wildly twisting canyons were created ages ago when a giant serpent squirmed its way south. Today, many visitors view the canyons aboard "ducks"— amphibious trucks that leave the highway to float on the river. But to a certain degree, "the Dells" is a victim of its own beauty. Every summer tourists flock to the area's souvenir shops, hot-dog stands, and gaudy amusement parks. Many visitors complain that this carnival atmosphere mars the region's natural splendor.

Eau Claire and Chippewa Falls lie along the Chippewa River. Early French explorers, impressed by the clarity of the river, named one of their camps Eau Claire, meaning "clear water," and the name stuck. Eau Claire is the home of the Chippewa Valley Museum which displays historical items. At one time the largest

The Wisconsin River carved out the canyons and gorges of the Wisconsin Dells.

sawmill in the state operated at Chippewa Falls. Today, the Cook-Rutledge Mansion, which once was the home of the town's leading lumber baron, is a museum open to the public.

Residents of La Crosse hail it as an "all-American city." Prosperous and squeaky clean, one of its major industries is the G. Heileman brewery, which competes with Milwaukee companies for much of the nation's beer trade. Situated on and near the majestic bluffs of the Mississippi River, La Crosse is one of Wisconsin's most scenic cities. Visitors there can enjoy a two-hour tour of the river aboard a restored paddle-wheel steamer.

Highway 35 is Wisconsin's section of the Great River Road, which runs from the Gulf of Mexico to Minnesota along the course of the Mississippi River. In Wisconsin, the road winds from Prairie du Chien north to Prescott. The Mississippi is normally thought of as a southern river, but though narrower, it is even lovelier in the north. The Great River Road climbs up bluffs and crosses floodplains. Only rarely do motorists lose sight of the river. An imaginative tourist can picture the river as it was a century and a half ago, alive with paddle-wheel steamboats and serving as the superhighway of the frontier.

Wilson's store in Ephraim, a popular summer gathering place, is a Door County landmark.

THE NORTH

The Door Peninsula, or Door County, has more than 250 miles (400 kilometers) of shoreline. The 70-mile- (112-kilometer-) long peninsula also has five state parks, giving it the greatest concentration of wilderness areas in the state. Beautiful Peninsula State Park, surrounded on three sides by the waters of Green Bay, contains 3,763 acres (1,523 hectares) of forest, campgrounds, and an eighteen-hole golf course. The limestone bluffs overlooking the bay offer spectacular views. Hiking trails at Newport State Park at the tip of the peninsula lead to lonely, windswept beaches.

Because of its shoreline, parks, and quaint towns, Door County is a popular spot for tourists. Jacksonport and Bailey's Harbor, on the Lake Michigan side of the peninsula, and Egg Harbor, Fish Creek, Sister Bay, and Ellison Bay on the Green Bay side, are some of the charming communities that hug the shore. At the tip of the Door Peninsula lies Washington Island, which can be reached only by ferry. The island, a coarse but beautiful place of farms, beaches, and woods, is home to the country's oldest Icelandic community.

One of Wisconsin's scenic wonders is Big Manitou Falls on the Black River in Pattison State Park just south of Superior. It is the highest of the state's hundreds of waterfalls.

To the west spreads the Nicolet National Forest, which is named for the first white man known to set foot on Wisconsin's soil. The thick forest is dotted with sparkling lakes. Countless lakes speckle the landscape near Rhinelander and Eagle River. Lake Julia provides a gorgeous setting for Nicolet College in Rhinelander. A short distance west there sprawls another dense woodland, the Chequamegon National Forest. Hayward and Cable, to the west, are the starting and ending points of the American Birkebeiner. This is the largest cross-country ski race in North America.

Towns and farms are fewer along the Lake Superior shoreline. Here, when the moon is full, the howl of the timber wolf sometimes pierces the night. Centuries ago, this Lake Superior region was a battleground between the Chippewa and the Fox. Today, tourists shop at the Chippewa Indian Arts and Crafts Center which is shaped like a modernistic tepee. The Red Cliff Indian Reservation lies nearby.

Bayfield, on the Lake Superior shore, looks surprisingly like a New England town. From its docks, ferries take visitors to the Apostle Islands. This island group is so lovely that it has been declared a National Lakeshore. To preserve its natural setting, nothing may be built there. There are twenty-two islands in the group, but legends claim that French explorers could see only twelve of them from the shore. Hence, they called them the Apostles, after the twelve followers of Jesus Christ. Madeline Island, which is not part of the National Lakeshore, has 150 permanent residents. Each year the island's population swells with as many as three thousand summer vacationers.

Superior is northern Wisconsin's largest city. It is a manufacturing center but most of its commerce comes from its port facilities. At Superior's busy waterfront, iron ore is loaded onto ships that take it to steel mills in lower Great Lakes cities. Superior also ships grain from the rich fields of midwestern America to hungry people halfway around the earth.

Superior is an appropriate place to end a journey in Wisconsin. Historically, it is a link between the Great Lakes and points west. The city clamors with industry, but no resident is more than an hour away from the forest hiking trail. The residents of Superior, like most Wisconsinites, live with one foot in the industrial world and the other in nature's wonderland.

WISCONSIN

1848

FACTS AT A GLANCE

GENERAL INFORMATION

Statehood: May 29, 1848, thirtieth state

Origin of Name: Named for the Wisconsin River, whose Chippewa name is translated as "the gathering of waters"

State Capital: Madison was selected as the first permanent territorial and then state capital; the territorial assembly first met in Madison in 1838, ten years before Wisconsin became a state. Temporary "capitals," or meeting sites, for the Wisconsin Territorial Legislature were near Belmont (now Leslie) and at Burlington (now part of Iowa).

State Nickname: "Badger State"; also called "America's Dairyland"

State Flag: The state flag was adopted in 1913. Centered on a dark blue field is the four-part Wisconsin shield symbolizing Wisconsin's agriculture, mining, navigation, and manufacturing. In its center is the United States shield. A sailor stands at the left of the Wisconsin shield, and a miner at the right. Above it is a badger and below are a horn of plenty and a pyramid of pig lead. The state motto, "Forward," and a band of thirteen stars for the thirteen original colonies are above and below. Above and below them are the name "Wisconsin" and "1848," the year of statehood.

State Motto: "Forward"

State Bird: Robin

State Flower: Wood violet

State Tree: Sugar maple

State Insect: Honeybee

State Mineral: Galena

State Rock: Red granite

State Animal: Badger (there are also an official State Domestic Animal, the Holstein dairy cow, and an official State Wildlife Animal, the white-tailed deer)

The Madison skyline from Lake Monona

State Symbol of Peace: Mourning dove

State Fossil: Trilobite

State Fish: Muskellunge

State Song: The football song "On Wisconsin!" written by William T. Purdy in 1909, was unofficially the state song until 1959. In that year, its melody and new first verse were adopted as the official song:

> On, Wisconsin! On, Wisconsin!
> Grand old badger state!
> We, thy loyal sons and daughters,
> Hail thee, good and great.
> On Wisconsin! On, Wisconsin!
> Champion of the right,
> "Forward," our motto—
> God will give thee might!

POPULATION

Population: 4,891,769, sixteenth among the states (1990 census)

Population Density: 90.1 people per sq. mi. (34.8 per km²)

Population Distribution: About two-thirds of the people live in cities or towns, while about one-third live in rural areas.

Milwaukee	628,088
Madison	191,262
Green Bay	96,466
Racine	84,298
Kenosha	80,352
Appleton	65,695
West Allis	63,221
Waukesha	56,958
Eau Claire	56,856

(Population figures according to 1990 census)

Population Growth: Wisconsin's population was twenty-five times greater in 1860 than in 1840. Miners and farmers from the eastern United States rushed to the productive and profitable mines and land of the new state. Between 1860 and 1900, Wisconsin's population increased steadily, if less dramatically. In the 1900s, the state's population has continued a steady increase. Between 1980 and 1990, Wisconsin experienced its smallest population increase—4 percent. The population of the entire country grew 9.8 percent. The list below shows the official national census figures for Wisconsin since 1840:

Year	Population
1840	30,945
1860	775,881
1880	1,315,497
1900	2,069,042
1920	2,632,067
1940	3,137,587
1950	3,434,575
1960	3,951,777
1970	4,417,933
1980	4,705,621
1990	4,891,769

Native Americans: The 1990 census reported Wisconsin's Native American population as 39,387. Native Americans live on reservations and in cities and towns throughout the state. The reservations occupy almost 405,000 acres (162,000 hectares) of land. More than three thousand Native Americans live on the Menominee Reservation. Nearly six thousand Native Americans live in Milwaukee.

GEOGRAPHY

Borders: Lake Superior and the Upper Peninsula of Michigan border Wisconsin on the north. Lake Michigan is Wisconsin's eastern border, Minnesota and Iowa are to the west, and Illinois is the southern border.

Highest Point: Timms Hill in Price County, 1,952 ft. (595 m) above sea level

Lowest Point: Lake Michigan's shoreline, 580 ft. (174 m) above sea level

Greatest Distances: North to south—320 mi. (512 km)
East to west—295 mi. (472 km)

Area: 56,154 sq. mi. (145,439 km²)

Rank in Area Among the States: Twenty-sixth

Rivers: The Mississippi River, which forms much of Wisconsin's western border, is the major navigable river in the state. Wisconsin has more than 20,000

mi. (32,000 km) of rivers. The longest river is the Wisconsin. From the northern highlands, it flows south and southwesterly 430 mi. (688 km) through the state until it joins the Mississippi just below Prairie du Chien. The Saint Croix, Chippewa, and La Crosse rivers also flow into the Mississippi in Wisconsin. The Rock River flows south into Illinois before it joins the Mississippi. Rivers that flow into Lake Michigan (or into Green Bay and then into Lake Michigan) include the Menominee, Milwaukee, Oconto, Peshtigo, and the Fox and its major tributary, the Wolf. In the far northwest, the Bad, Montreal, and Nemadji are short rivers that flow from the highlands directly north into Lake Superior.

Wisconsin's scenic wonders include hundreds of waterfalls. The highest is Big Manitou Falls (165 ft./49.5 m) at Pattison State Park near Superior. Wisconsin also boasts 2,444 trout streams—just over 9,000 mi. (14,400 km) of fishing if laid end-to-end—and 144 canoe rivers, or a 3,484-mi. (5,574-km) canoe trip if they were joined together.

Lakes: Within Wisconsin lie some fifteen thousand lakes. Lake Winnebago in Winnebago County is the largest at 137,708 acres (55,083 hectares); Big Green Lake in Green Lake County is the deepest, with depths of 229 ft. (68.7 m). Madison, Wisconsin's capital city, is beautified by Lake Mendota and its smaller sister lakes Monona, Waubesa, and Kegonsa. Other major lakes in Wisconsin are Lake Pepin at the Mississippi boundary, Lake Poygan in Winnebago County, Lake Koshkonong in Jefferson County, Shawano Lake in Shawano County, and Lake Geneva in Walworth County. Wisconsin's largest reservoirs and artificial lakes are Petenwell Lake and Castle Rock Lake, both in Juneau County; Lake Chippewa in Sawyer County; and Turtle-Flambeau Flowage in Iron County. Almost 3 percent of Wisconsin's total area consists of inland water. In addition to the larger lakes, hundreds of small but beautiful lakes dot the north. Vilas County has so many lakes that its total area is almost one-fifth water. Wisconsin's boundaries also include 679 mi. (1,086 km) of shoreline along lakes Michigan and Superior.

Topography: Geographers divide Wisconsin into five major topographic regions: the Lake Superior Lowlands, the Superior Uplands, the Western Uplands, the Great Lakes Plain, and the Central Plain.

The Superior Uplands or Northern Highlands include 15,000 sq. mi. (38,850 km²) of forested hills and hundreds of small lakes, land features left behind ten thousand years ago when the last glacier retreated. Wisconsin's highest elevations, including Timms Hill in Price County, are located here.

A smaller area of 1,250 sq. mi. (about 3,238 km²) called the Lake Superior Lowlands consists of the Apostle Islands in Lake Superior and sandy beaches that line the Lake Superior shore and extend 5-10 mi. (8-16 km) inland to end abruptly at steep cliffs.

The Western Uplands, 13,250 sq. mi. (34,318 km²) of deep valleys and narrow ridges along the Mississippi River, are called the Driftless Area because they were largely untouched by the drifting glaciers. Here the Mississippi River and its tributaries the Saint Croix and La Crosse rivers have carved out deep, scenic gorges in their course to the sea.

The Great Lakes Plain (also called the Eastern Ridges and Lowlands) begins in the north at the Door Peninsula and the Lake Michigan islands there and continues south along the sandy beaches and steep bluffs of the Lake Michigan shoreline, Wisconsin's eastern border. It extends westward to include the gently rolling plains

of the southeastern quarter of the state. The Great Lakes Plain, 13,500 sq. mi. (34,965) km²), contains Wisconsin's richest farmland and its heaviest population, the Milwaukee-Racine-Kenosha area. The glaciers left behind a "kettle-moraine" area northwest of Milwaukee that consists of "kettles," or holes, where buried ice boulders melted away and knobs where the glaciers deposited accumulated debris as they retreated.

The crescent-shaped Central Plain is 13,000 sq. mi. (33,670 km²) of land in the center of Wisconsin between the Western Uplands and the Great Lakes Plain, and below the Superior Uplands. It includes glaciated areas and driftless areas. The 7-mi. (11-km) stretch of Wisconsin River gorge called the Wisconsin Dells is in the Central Plain.

Climate: Wisconsin has warm summers; long, cold winters; and relatively low humidity. Sudden temperature changes are common because swift-moving windstorms sweep across the land with no high mountains to contain them. Temperatures range from average January temperatures of 10° F. (-12.2° C) in the north and 22° F. (-5.6° C) in the southeast to average July temperatures of 66° F. (19° C) in the north and 72° F. (22° C) in the southwest. Wisconsin's highest recorded temperature was 114° F. (46° C) at the Wisconsin Dells in July 1936; its lowest recorded temperature was -54° F. (-47° C) at Danbury in January 1922. Lake Michigan and Lake Superior modify temperature and some climate extremes for areas within a few miles of the lakeshore. Almost 50 percent of Wisconsin's annual precipitation occurs during summer. Southern Wisconsin averages 30 in. (76 cm) of annual precipitation, while northern Wisconsin might receive 50-60 in. (125-150 cm) and more. Annual snowfall averages 30 in. (76 cm) in the south, but Iron County in the north might get up to 100 in. (254 cm) of snow. Many streams and smaller lakes are frozen from December through April.

113

Trillium (above) and marsh marigolds (inset) are among the hundreds of varieties of wildflowers that grow in Wisconsin.

NATURE

Trees: Black ash, beech, aspen, hickory, white elm, sugar maple, silver maple, mountain maple, yellow birch, bur oak, black oak, white oak, and red oak are common hardwood trees in Wisconsin. Balsam fir, hemlock, white pine, jack pine, spruce, tamarack, white cedar, and cottonwood are typical softwood trees.

Wild Plants: Wild black currant, blueberry, huckleberry, Juneberry, and raspberry shrubs, pink trailing arbutus, some twenty varieties of violet, forty-five species of orchid (including several endangered species), wild aster, goldenrod, fireweed, and numerous spring and fall wildflowers

Animals: black bear, white-tailed deer, coyote, red fox, gray fox, gray wolf, beaver, muskrat, mink, skunk, prairie mice, gopher, badger, chipmunk, raccoon, woodchuck, porcupine

Birds: Wisconsin has over 330 native bird species. Game birds include ducks, geese, jacksnipes, partridge, quail, pheasant, grouse, and woodcocks. Marshland and lake birds include loons, bittern, black tern, and coots. Woodland and song birds include chickadees, nuthatches, robins, swallows, warblers, and wrens.

Fish: Muskellunge, bass, pickerel, pike, sturgeon, trout, salmon, and perch and other panfish are sport fish. Lake trout, whitefish, herring, and perch from Lake Michigan and Superior, and catfish and bass from the Mississippi River are fished commercially.

GOVERNMENT

The government of Wisconsin, like the federal government, is divided into three branches—legislative, executive, and judicial.

The state's legislative branch, the Wisconsin legislature, is made up of a Senate with thirty-three members and an Assembly with ninety-nine members. The legislature creates new laws, rescinds or revises old ones, and works with the governor to prepare the state budget. Voters elect senators to four-year terms, and representatives to the Assembly for two-year terms. The legislature meets annually in January for an unlimited session.

The executive branch, headed by the governor, administers the law. The governor is elected to a four-year term. There is no limit to the number of terms a governor may serve. The lieutenant governor, secretary of state, attorney general, treasurer, and state superintendent of public instruction also are elected by the people to four-year terms. The state constitution gives the governor the authority to veto or approve laws passed by the legislature, to grant pardons and executive clemency, to deliver state-of-the-state and budget messages to the legislature, and to veto an entire bill, or when appropriation of funds is requested in a bill, parts of the bill. The governor also serves as commander-in-chief of the state militia, and can call emergency sessions of the state legislature.

The judicial branch consists of a seven-member supreme court, a twelve-member court of appeals, sixty-nine circuit courts, and more than two hundred municipal courts. All judges are elected on a nonpartisan basis in the April election. Supreme court justices are elected for ten-year terms. Justices of the court of appeals are elected to six-year terms. They usually hear cases in three-member panels. The circuit courts are the trial courts. The municipal courts have jurisdiction on local ordinances. Municipal court judges are elected for two to four years, as specified locally.

Number of Counties: 72

U.S. Representatives: 9

Electoral Votes: 11

Voting Qualifications: Citizens of sound mind at least eighteen years of age, with six months residency in the state and ten days residency in the election district

EDUCATION

Wisconsin spends about $4.5 billion on public education each year. Wisconsin's public schools are directed by the superintendent of public instruction, who is elected to a four-year term. Attendance is required of all children aged six through fifteen. In districts with a vocational school, attendance is required until age eighteen or completion of the twelfth grade. There are about 432 school districts in the state. Total student enrollment in kindergarten through grade twelve is about 767,542 in public schools and 153,661 in private schools.

Wisconsin has about sixty-two institutions (including branches) of higher learning. About thirty are public, with about 186,700 full-time students. The thirty-two private institutions have about 31,000 full-time students enrolled. The University of Wisconsin was founded in Madison in 1848 and now has campuses in Eau Claire, Green Bay, La Crosse, Milwaukee, Oshkosh, Kenosha (Parkside), Platteville, River Falls, Stevens Point, Menominee (Stout), Superior, and Whitewater. There are about 80,000 men and 81,000 women enrolled in the Wisconsin state university system. In addition, public vocational, technical, and adult-education schools enroll over 461,000 students. The largest number (21,356) is enrolled at Milwaukee Area Technical College.

Marquette University in Milwaukee is the state's largest private university. Carroll College in Waukesha is the state's oldest private college. Other private colleges and universities include Lawrence University in Appleton, and Beloit, Ripon, Carthage, and Saint Norbert colleges. Specialized private schools include the Milwaukee School of Engineering.

ECONOMY AND INDUSTRY

Principal Products

Agriculture: Dairy products, livestock, hay, sweet corn, beets, green peas, snap beans, cranberries, tart cherries, apples, oats, soybeans, wheat, barley

Manufacturing: Nonelectric machinery, processed foods, plumbing fixtures, farm machinery, paper products, electric equipment, medical and laboratory supplies, automobiles, trucks and car parts, lumber, paper pulp, cheese and processed dairy products, malt beverages

Natural Resources: Fertile soil, forests, lakes and rivers, sand and gravel, iron, lead, zinc, sulfide, basalt, clay, peat, quartzite, sandstone

Business and Trade: Manufacturing provides more than 22 percent of the total state employment and 36 percent of all earnings. More than eight thousand factories produce over $22 billion in goods each year. Wisconsin ranks first in the nation in production of paper, aluminum utensils, outboard motors, lawn mowers, motorcycles, snowmobile engines, and paper products. Automobiles, plumbing fixtures, and farm machinery are important Wisconsin products.

Wisconsin, "America's Dairyland," ranks first nationwide in production of milk, butter, and cheese. The state also ranks high in production of all other dairy products, as well as poultry, eggs, and meat. Wisconsin produces about 40 percent of the nation's cranberries and 90 percent of its ginseng. Other major agricultural products are beets, green peas, snap beans, cabbage for processing, spearmint, and peppermint.

Tourism is an important service industry. Wisconsin's state parks alone host about nine million visitors each year.

Milwaukee, the state's largest city, is its major trade center. In 1977 Milwaukee County had 23 percent of Wisconsin's wholesale firms and 42 percent of its trade volume. J.C. Penney, the large mail-order house and retail chain, has its home office in Milwaukee.

Communication: Wisconsin has about 325 newspapers, of which just over 10 percent are dailies. Newspapers with the largest circulation are the *Milwaukee Journal*, the *Milwaukee Sentinel*, the *Green Bay Press Gazette*, and the *Wisconsin State Journal* in Madison. The *Green-Bay Intelligencer*, Wisconsin's first newspaper, was founded in 1833. The *Wiskonsin-Banner*, published in Milwaukee in 1844, was the state's first German-language newspaper. In 1969, *La Guardia*, a Spanish-English newspaper, was founded in Milwaukee. The Wisconsin Press Association (now the Wisconsin Newspaper Association), founded in 1853, was the first state news service in the nation.

Wisconsin has about 225 radio stations. The University of Wisconsin radio station was first licensed in 1916. There are 22 commercial television stations in the state and 8 educational television stations. WTMJ-TV, Wisconsin's first television station, began broadcasting in Milwaukee in 1947.

Transportation: Wisconsin has about 108,000 mi. (172,800 km) of roads and highways. Of these, 95 percent are paved. There are some 5,000 mi. (8,000 km) of railroad track in Wisconsin, and nineteen railroad lines. Ten cities have passenger service. Railroad freight traffic totals nearly 100 million short tons (about 90 million metric tons) and over $476 million each year. Wisconsin's more than 600 airports include 381 privately owned and 96 publicly owned fields, plus military, helicopter, and seaplane bases. The state's largest airport is Mitchell Field in Milwaukee. Other cities served by commercial airlines include Green Bay, Appleton, and Madison.

Milwaukee is a major Great Lakes port. Since the completion of the St. Lawrence Seaway in 1959, Milwaukee, Green Bay, Kenosha, Racine, Manitowoc, Superior, and other Wisconsin cities are visited by oceangoing traffic. Each year Wisconsin's ports service nearly one million passengers and handle about 35 million short tons (31.7 million metric tons) of freight. Automobile ferries cross Lake Michigan between Ludington, Michigan, and Kewaunee, Manitowoc, and Milwaukee. A ferry also crosses between Kewaunee and Frankfort, Michigan.

SOCIAL AND CULTURAL LIFE

Museums: The Milwaukee Public Museum is the state's largest museum of natural science, applied science, and human history. It is noted for its large collection of prehistoric Indian tools and weapons. Exhibits range from the Age of Dinosaurs to the Information Age of computerized robots. The Milwaukee Art Museum, housed in the War Memorial along Lake Michigan, has a large permanent collection ranging from the ancient to the modern. The Milwaukee Art Center, founded in 1888, specializes in European works from the seventeenth through nineteenth centuries. The Charles Allis Art Library in Milwaukee houses collections of Chinese porcelains, French antiques, and nineteenth-century American landscapes. Other Wisconsin museums include the Elvehjem Museum of Art and the Madison Art Center in Madison, the Theodore Lyman Wright Art Center at Beloit College, and the Blakely Museum in Fond du Lac. Specialized museums include the Dard Hunter Paper Museum in Appleton, the Museum of Medical Progress in Prairie du Chien, the Rhinelander Logging Museum in Rhinelander, and the Farm and Draft Museum in Cassville.

Libraries: Wisconsin has about 360 public libraries, organized into seventeen regional library systems. The Wisconsin Free Library Commission sponsors traveling libraries that visit all parts of the state. The Milwaukee Public Library and the University of Wisconsin Library at Madison are the state's largest. The State Historical Society of Wisconsin at Madison has about 200,000 books and 300,000 documents concerning the history of Wisconsin.

Performing Arts: The Milwaukee Symphony Orchestra under music director Zdenek Macal gives nearly two hundred concerts a year. The Florentine Opera Company, in Milwaukee, was founded in 1934. The Milwaukee Ballet Company, a nationally acclaimed dance company, performs classical and contemporary dance at the Milwaukee Performing Arts Center. The Milwaukee Repertory Theater is a professional acting group that has been performing traditional and contemporary plays since 1952. The American Players Theater, a professional arts theater located in Spring Green, performs plays of Shakespeare, Chekhov, and other masters from July through October. The Skylight Comic Opera in Milwaukee performs operas and operettas from Mozart to Gilbert and Sullivan. Broadway and popular musicals are performed at the Melody Top Theater in Milwaukee, which also has a Children's Theater, and at The Fireside Restaurant and Playhouse in Fort Atkinson. Films, lectures, and concerts are presented throughout the year at colleges and universities around the state.

Sports and Recreation: Wisconsin has three professional athletic teams. Baseball is played at Milwaukee County Stadium, the home of the Milwaukee Brewers of the American League. The Milwaukee Bucks of the National Basketball Association (NBA) play at the Mecca Arena in Milwaukee. Lambeau Field, in Green Bay, is the home of the Green Bay Packers of the National Football League (NFL). The University of Wisconsin at Madison is a member of the Big Ten Athletic Conference. Marquette University in Milwaukee is a former National Collegiate Athletic Association (NCAA) champion in basketball. Road America at Elkhart Lake is host to championship auto races. The American Birkebeiner cross-country ski race is run from Hayward to Cable each winter.

The Milwaukee County Zoo has no cages. Animals are exhibited in settings as similar as possible to their natural habitats.

At the Mitchell Park Horticultural Conservatory in Milwaukee, three huge glass domes contain tropical, arid, and seasonal plant displays. Each dome is almost fifty yards (about forty-six meters) in diameter and seventy feet (twenty-one meters) tall. Featured are Easter and Christmas shows with masses of lilies and poinsettias on display. The Boerner Botanical Garden in Hales Corners displays roses, perennials, wildflowers, annuals, herbs, and an arboretum.

Outdoor sports enthusiasts may choose among dozens of activities in Wisconsin, from rafting in the rapids of the Wolf River near the Wisconsin Dells (left) to skiing in the American Birkebeiner cross-country race from Hayward to Cable (above).

Wisconsin's 14,000 lakes and 26,000 mi. (41,600 km) of rivers and streams provide year-round recreation. Anglers fish for northern pike, walleyes, yellow perch, small- and large-mouth bass, bluegills, crappies, rainbow trout, muskellunge (muskies), and coho salmon. Canoeing, sailing, motorboating, and water skiing are popular as are houseboat vacations and boat tours. Wisconsin has seven state bicycle trails, built on abandoned railroad corridors. The Elroy-Sparta bike trail passes through three abandoned railway tunnels.

Wisconsin has two national forests, Chequamegon and Nicolet, and one National Lakeshore area, the Apostle Islands in Lake Superior. Two National Parkways are shared by Wisconsin and Minnesota: the Saint Croix National Scenic River and the Lower Saint Croix National Scenic River. The state also has ten state forests, totaling 476,004 acres (190,402 hectares), and fifty-five state parks, totaling 61,433 acres (24,577 hectares).

At Devil's Lake State Park, 500-foot (150-meter) bluffs adjoin a 360-acre (144-hectare) lake. Peninsula State Park in Door County is noted for autumn leaf color. Governor Dodge State Park is in Wisconsin's Driftless Area. High Cliffs State Park overlooks Lake Winnebago. At Kettle Moraine State Parks, North and South, the glaciers left rolling hills and small, deep lakes.

Historic Sites and Landmarks:

Annunciation Greek Orthodox Church, in Wauwatosa was the last major building designed by Frank Lloyd Wright. It is a blue-domed Byzantine-style edifice.

Heritage Hill State Park, in Green Bay is a forty-eight acre (about nineteen hectares) site containing twenty-two structures from early Wisconsin history. The military, agricultural, pioneer, and small-town heritage of early Wisconsin are preserved in historical settings.

Oneida Nation Museum in Oneida contains displays explaining the history of the League of the Iroquois, and the move from New York State to Wisconsin. On display are a reconstructed Oneida village and a medicinal herb garden.

Circus World Museum in Baraboo is a forty-acre (sixteen-hectare) site in the city where the Ringling Brothers started their circus. Many original buildings remain and are used by the museum. Circus animals, colorful parades, calliope music, circus performances, and clowns can also be seen.

Madeline Island Historical Museum is in the village of La Pointe on Madeline Island, the largest of the Apostle Islands at the northernmost tip of Wisconsin. The museum building is actually four different log structures: the old town jail; the Old Sailors' Home; a barn; and a building once used by John Jacob Astor's American Fur Trading Company. The museum contains displays and artifacts relating to local history, especially the history of the early fur trade.

The Old Wade House in Greenbush was built in 1851 by Sylvanus Wade. For many years it was an inn on the Old Sheboygan and Fond du Lac Plank Road. But with the coming of the railroad after the Civil War, its importance declined. Today the Wade House, Sylvanus Wade's blacksmith shop, and the nearby Charles Robinson House have been completely restored. Costumed employees still perform daily chores of the original inn, such as spinning, weaving, candle and soap making, blacksmithing and grooming of horses. The Wesley W. Jung Carriage Museum features one of America's best collections of horse-drawn carriages and working wagons.

Old World Wisconsin, near Eagle, is an outdoor museum celebrating Wisconsin's ethnic heritage. More than forty buildings from all over Wisconsin have been assembled at this state park. Originally built by early immigrants to Wisconsin, these buildings include homes, churches, schools, places of business, and community buildings. Also among the buildings are Norwegian, Finnish, Danish, Swiss, German, and Yankee farmhouses. An authentically costumed staff performs the daily chores of the nineteenth century.

Pendarvis, in Mineral Point, is a group of restored stone and log houses built by Cornish miners who came to the area in the 1830s and 1840s to mine lead. The houses on Shake Rag Street, furnished with nineteenth-century antiques and lead-mining artifacts, offer a glimpse into the lives of these miners and their families. The Merry Christmas Mine property across the street may also be toured.

Stonefield Village, near Cassville, is a re-creation of a turn-of-the-century village where the blacksmith still pounds glowing iron with his hammer and the print shop still publishes the *Stonefield Gazette*. Just beyond the village is the State Farm Museum.

Villa Louis, in Prairie du Chien, is a lavish mansion built on a former Indian burial mound for Hercules Dousman in 1870 and restored by the Dousman family in the 1930s. Nearby, an exhibit of the fur trade in the Upper Mississippi Valley is on display in the recently opened *Astor Fur Warehouse*.

The beautiful Villa Louis mansion in Prairie du Chien was built in 1870.

Other Interesting Places to Visit

The Captain Frederick Pabst Mansion in Milwaukee is a thirty-seven-room house with twelve baths and fourteen fireplaces. Built for Frederick Pabst, of "Pabst Blue Ribbon Beer" fame, it is a showplace of wood carvings by the Matthews brothers and ornamental ironwork by Cyril Colnik.

Cave of the Mounds, between Mount Horeb and Blue Mounds, features hundreds of colorful stone formations in fourteen rooms of the cavern.

Door County, the peninsula resort area in northeastern Wisconsin, has five state parks and more than 250 miles (400 kilometers) of shoreline on Lake Michigan.

Eagle Cave, near Blue River, is Wisconsin's largest onyx cave. Guided tours of the cave and in-cave camping are offered, as well as swimming, fishing, hiking, horseback riding, canoeing, and hayrides in the natural park at the site.

Green Meadows Farm, near Waterford, has a modern dairy barn where milking demonstrations are given. Twenty animal areas feature goats, sheep, rabbits, turkeys, ducks, pigs, chickens, and horses. There are hayrides, pony rides, sleigh rides, nature trails, and picnic areas.

House on the Rock, a few miles north of Dodgeville, is a twenty-two-room house built atop a huge rock 450 feet (135 meters) in height. It has antiques, giant music boxes, six fireplaces, seven pools, and magnificent views of the countryside.

The Octagon House in Watertown (above) was built before the Civil War. A restored Norwegian homestead of the 1800s (right) and several other Scandinavian pioneer houses stand on the grounds of Little Norway.

Johnson Wax Golden Rondelle Guest Relations Center, in Racine, is the worldwide headquarters of the S.C. Johnson and Son Company. It was designed by the famed architect Frank Lloyd Wright.

Lake Geneva, in south-central Wisconsin, is a popular resort area. Surrounding the lake are magnificent mansions that can be viewed during a boat tour around the lake.

Little Norway, near Mount Horeb, is a restored Norwegian homestead of the early 1800s. The site has many furnished Scandinavian pioneer houses.

The Mining Museum, in Platteville, traces the history of lead and zinc mining in the Upper Mississippi Valley. A guided tour includes a walk down into Bevans Lead, an 1845 lead mine, and a train ride around the museum grounds in ore cars pulled by a 1931 mine locomotive.

The Rollo Jamison Museum, in Platteville, contains more than twenty thousand items from the everyday lives of people at the beginning of the twentieth century.

The Octagon House and First Kindergarten are in Watertown. The Octagon House is one of the largest single-family residences built in Wisconsin prior to the Civil War. It is a five-story structure containing fifty-seven rooms. Also on the grounds is the restored building that contained the first kindergarten in the United States, founded by Margarethe Schurz in 1856.

Taliesin, near Spring Green, was the country home of architect Frank Lloyd Wright. It is now a school and a memorial to Wright's life and work.

Wisconsin Dells, in Adams, Columbia, Juneau, and Sauk counties, is a seven-mile (about eleven-kilometer) channel of rock formations created by the Wisconsin River as it flowed through the surrounding soft sandstone.

Wisconsin State Capitol in Madison is a Roman Renaissance structure designed by George Post in 1906. Only two inches (about five centimeters) shorter than the United States Capitol in Washington, D.C., after which it was modeled, it is situated between lakes Mendota and Monona, where it dominates the Madison skyline.

IMPORTANT DATES

c. 10,000 B.C.—Last glaciers retreat north across Wisconsin

300 B.C.-A.D. 500—Huge burial mounds at the confluence of the Mississippi and Wisconsin rivers, near Prairie du Chien, are built by people of the Hopewell Culture

800-1600s—Fox, Sauk, and Winnebago people occupy what is now Wisconsin

1634—Jean Nicolet, seeking a northwest passage, becomes first white man known to reach Wisconsin

1654-1659—Pierre-Esprit, Sieur de Radisson, and Médard Chouart, Sieur des Groseillers, French fur traders, arrive in Wisconsin

1661—Father René Ménard becomes the first Roman Catholic missionary to Wisconsin Indians

1672—Wisconsin becomes part of New France

1673—Louis Jolliet and Pere Jacques Marquette travel through Wisconsin and become the first white people to report seeing the Mississippi River

1718—French build a fort at Green Bay

c. 1745—Charles de Langlade establishes first permanent settlement at Green Bay

1763—British defeat French; Wisconsin becomes part of British territory under Treaty of Paris

1774—Wisconsin becomes part of British province of Quebec

1783—Wisconsin becomes part of United States under Second Treaty of Paris

1787—Wisconsin becomes part of Northwest Territory

1800—Wisconsin included in Indiana Territory

1809—Wisconsin included in Illinois Territory

1814—United States flag flies over Wisconsin for the first time, Fort Shelby, Prairie du Chien

1815—Fort Shelby, captured by British during War of 1812, is regained by the United States and then abandoned

1816—John Jacob Astor's American Fur Company begins operating in Wisconsin

1818—Soloman Juneau buys a trading post at Milwaukee

1822—Indians from New York State begin to move into Wisconsin

1824—Judge James Doty holds the first United States Circuit Court session in Wisconsin, at Green Bay

1825—Erie Canal opens, easing migration to the West

1832—Black Hawk War ends; whites now control all Wisconsin land

1833—Wisconsin's first newspaper, the *Green Bay Intelligencer,* is established

1835—First steamboat arrives in Milwaukee; first bank in Wisconsin opens in Green Bay

1836—Territory of Wisconsin created

1839—Three towns consolidate to become Milwaukee

1846—Solomon Juneau elected first mayor of Milwaukee; Congress passes enabling act allowing statehood for Wisconsin

1848—Constitution ratified, March 13; Wisconsin becomes the thirtieth state; University of Wisconsin founded; state public school system created

1851—Wisconsin's first railroad, from Milwaukee to Waukesha, opens; first Wisconsin State Fair held

1854—Republican party holds early meetings at Ripon

1856—Margarethe Schurz establishes first United States kindergarten, at Watertown

1866—First state normal school opens, at Platteville

1868—Christopher Latham Sholes patents the first practical typewriter

1871—Peshtigo fire kills twelve hundred people

1872 — Wisconsin Dairymen's Association founded at Watertown

1875 — Women declared eligible to vote for school offices; city of Oshkosh nearly destroyed by fire

1884 — Ringling Brothers Circus founded in Baraboo

1885 — High-grade iron ore discovered in the Gogebic Range

1900 — Robert M. La Follette, Sr. elected governor

1903 — Wisconsin adopts nation's first mandatory primary elections

1905 — Wisconsin state civil service law established

1911 — First Wisconsin state income–tax law passed

1917 — Wisconsin becomes first state to identify highways by number; new State Capitol completed

1924 — La Follette wins Wisconsin's presidential vote as Progressive party candidate

1925 — La Follette dies; his son, Robert M. La Follette, Jr., is elected to the Senate in his place

1931-1932 — Wisconsin enacts first state unemployment–compensation law in nation

1946 — Wisconsin Progressive party dissolved and rejoins Republican party

1947 — First Wisconsin television station, WTMJ-TV, begins broadcasting from Milwaukee

1957 — Senator Joseph McCarthy dies; Milwaukee Braves baseball team wins World Series; William Proxmire elected to United States Senate for the first time

1960 — Dena Smith, elected state treasurer, becomes first woman elected to Wisconsin statewide office

1962 — Kohler Company strike, which began in 1954, ends

1967 — Civil-rights demonstrators march for an open-housing ordinance in Milwaukee

1970 — Building at the University of Wisconsin is bombed, one person killed

1971 — University of Wisconsin consolidates thirteen campuses and fourteen two-year schools

1972 — Age of majority lowered from twenty-one to eighteen; Milwaukee Brewers baseball team founded

1976 — United States District Court orders integration of Milwaukee schools

1977 — State employment strike lasts fifteen days

1983 — Minimum drinking age raised to nineteen

1986 — Floods following a violent rainstorm in Milwaukee kill two persons, swamp ten thousand houses, and cause $27 million in property damage

IMPORTANT PEOPLE

SHIRLEY ABRAHAMSON

JOHN BARDEEN

Shirley S. Abrahamson (1933-   ), lawyer and jurist; first woman ever appointed (1976) and then elected (1979) to Wisconsin Supreme Court

Claude Jean Allouez (1622-1689), French Jesuit missionary; first European known to travel through remote areas of Great Lakes and upper Mississippi Valley

Stephen Moulton Babcock (1843-1931), educator (University of Wisconsin) and agricultural chemist; developed the test to determine the amount of butterfat in dairy products (1890)

John Bardeen (1908-   ), born in Madison; physicist; helped develop the transistor and the superconductivity theory; first person to win two Nobel Prizes in physics (1956 and 1972)

Helen Barnhill (1937-   ), president of Barnhill-Hayes, Inc., a Milwaukee management-consulting firm specializing in human-resources management; served as national president of United Church of Christ

Victor Louis Berger (1860-1929), political leader and editor; lived in Milwaukee from age of twenty; with Eugene Debs, founded the Socialist party (1908); elected to United States House of Representatives (1910, 1918, 1923)

Black Hawk (1767-1838), Sauk Indian leader; resisted white settlers taking over lands in Wisconsin and Illinois; defeated by United States militia in the Battle of Bad Axe during Black Hawk War (1838)

Jerome Increase Case (1819-1891), manufacturerer; developed mechanical farming machinery that helped replace hand tools; founded the J.I. Case Company, manufacturer of agricultural implements, in Racine

Maureen Daly (1921-   ), grew up in Fond du Lac; novelist; author of *Seventeenth Summer* (1942), a classic novel of teenage romance, and other novels

Ada Deer (1935-   ), born on Menominee Indian Reservation, Wisconsin; educator and activist; gained national recognition for role in restoration of Menominee Indians to reservation status; spokesperson for DRUMS (Determination of the Rights and Unity of Menominee Shareholders); Native American Studies lecturer at University of Wisconsin-Madison

Edna Ferber (1885-1968), novelist and dramatist; grew up in Appleton; awarded Pulitzer Prize for *So Big* (1925); other novels, many of which became motion pictures, include *Show Boat* (1926), *Giant* (1952), *Ice Palace* (1958)

EDNA FERBER

Lynn Fontanne (1887-1983), actress; maintained home in Genesee Depot; with her husband Alfred Lunt, formed one of the country's most-beloved acting teams

Zona Gale (1874-1938), born in Portage; author; advocate of feminism, progressive political ideas, and racial equality; awarded 1921 Pulitzer Prize for dramatization of her novel *Miss Lulu Bett*

Arnold Lucius Gesell (1880-1961), born in Alma; psychologist; pioneer in scientific study of child development

ARNOLD GESELL

Ezekiel Gillespie (1818-1892), probably born a slave; lived in Milwaukee by 1852; as a result of a civil-rights case taken to the Wisconsin Supreme Court in his name, the court ruled that blacks had the right to vote in Wisconsin; one of the founders of the first African Methodist Episcopal Church in Milwaukee

James E. Groppi (1930-1985), born in Milwaukee; cleric and social activist; former Roman Catholic priest active in civil-rights causes

Médard Chouart, Sieur des Groseilliers (1618?-1696?), French fur trader and explorer; with his brother-in-law Radisson, first European to identify Chequamegon Bay

JAMES E. GROPPI

Agoston Haraszthy de Mokcsa (1812?-1869?), Hungarian count who founded Sauk City (c. 1841)

Cordelia Harvey (1824-1895), humanitarian; called the "Wisconsin Angel" because of her visits to hospitalized Civil War soldiers; led efforts to establish three military hospitals in Wisconsin

Marguerite Henry (1902-   ), born in Milwaukee; writer; author of *Misty of Chincoteague, Justin Morgan Had a Horse*, and other classic children's books about life with horses

Woodrow Charles (Woody) Herman (1913-   ), born in Milwaukee; jazz musician and bandleader

WOODY HERMAN

ELROY HIRSCH

HARRY HOUDINI

H.V. KALTENBORN

GEORGE F. KENNAN

Hildegarde (Sell) (1906-   ), born in Adell; singer, radio personality; introduced ''April in Paris'' and ''Wunderbar''

Elroy (Crazy Legs) Hirsch (1923-   ), born in Wausau; college and professional athlete; starred in the film *Crazylegs, All-American* (1953); elected to the Professional Football Hall of Fame (1968); Athletic Director of University of Wisconsin (1969-1986)

Daniel Webster Hoan (1881-1961), born in Waukesha; Socialist political leader; mayor of Milwaukee (1916-1940)

William Dempster Hoard (1836-1918), publisher, farmer, politician; cofounder of Wisconsin Dairymen's Association (1854); founded *Hoard's Dairyman* (1885); governor of Wisconsin (1889-90)

Harry Houdini (1874-1926), born Erich Weiss in Hungary; magician and escape artist; grew up in Appleton; one of the most accomplished escape artists of all times; starred in silent films; crusaded against fake spiritualists

Vinnie Ream Hoxie (1847-1914), born in Madison; sculptor; created the Abraham Lincoln statue in United States Capitol Rotunda and other sculptures in the Washington, D.C., area; created figure *The West* in the Wisconsin State Capitol

Samuel C. Johnson (1833-1919), industrialist; founded S.C. Johnson & Son Company (Johnson Wax), at Racine

Solomon Laurent Juneau (1793-1856), fur trader and political leader; with his family, Milwaukee area's first permanent white settler (1818); first mayor of Milwaukee (1846)

Hans von (H.V.) Kaltenborn (1878-1965), born in Milwaukee; broadcaster; broadcast radio news and commentary (1922-65)

George Frost Kennan (1904-   ), born in Milwaukee; diplomat and historian; coined the term ''containment'' to describe United States policy toward the Soviet Union after World War II; prizewinning writer on foreign policy

Walter Jodok Kohler, Sr. (1875-1940), born in Sheboygan; manufacturer and political leader; founded The Kohler Company, manufacturers of plumbing equipment; planned and built a model garden community for company workers; governor of Wisconsin (1929-1931)

Belle Case La Follette (1859-1931), born in Summit; attorney, journalist, social activist; first woman to graduate from University of Wisconsin Law School; with her husband, Robert M. La Follette, Sr., founded *La Follette's Magazine* (1909), active in the Women's Peace Party during World War I and Women's Committee for Disarmament after that war

Philip Fox La Follette (1897-1965), born in Madison; lawyer and political leader; with his brother, Robert M. La Follette, Jr., organized the Progressive political party (founded by their father) in Wisconsin; governor of Wisconsin (1931-33, 1935-39)

Robert Marion (Fighting Bob) La Follette, Sr. (1855-1925), born in Primrose; political leader; founded Progressive political party (1904); devoted his career to government and political reform in Wisconsin and the nation; governor of Wisconsin (1901-1905); United States senator (1906-25); opposed United States entry into World War I (1917); carried Wisconsin and won 17 percent of nation's vote as Progressive presidential candidate (1924)

Robert Marion La Follette, Jr. (1895-1953), born in Madison; lawyer and political leader; authority on tax legislation and activist on behalf of labor and civil liberties; upon his father's death became United States senator (1925-47)

Earl (Curly) Lambeau (1898-1965), professional football coach; founder and coach of the Green Bay Packers; instrumental in establishing the National Football League (1921)

Wladziu Valentino Liberace (1919-1987), born in West Allis; pianist; television and stage performer noted for flamboyant versions of classic and contemporary music

Ben Logan (1920-   ), born near Seneca; author; described his Wisconsin boyhood in *The Land Remembers* (1975)

Vince Lombardi (1913-1970), professional football coach; coach of Green Bay Packers, (1959-68); team won five league titles and Super Bowls I and II (1967 and 1968)

Patrick J. Lucey (1918-   ), born in La Crosse; political leader; governor of Wisconsin (1971-77); United States ambassador to Mexico (1977-79)

Alfred Lunt (1893-1977), born in Milwaukee; actor; with his wife, Lynn Fontanne, formed one of America's most-beloved acting teams; won Emmy Award for television drama *The Magnificent Yankee* (1965); awarded Presidential Medal of Honor

Frederic March (1897-1975), born Frederick Bickel in Racine; actor; won Academy Awards for roles in the films *Dr. Jekyll and Mr. Hyde* (1932) and *The Best Years of our Lives* (1946)

Joseph Raymond McCarthy (1908-1957), born in Grand Chute; political leader; United States senator (1947-57); launched a severe anti-Communist crusade that led to his censure in the Senate (1954); its harsh methods have come to be known as "McCarthyism"

Golda Meir (1893-1978), political leader; spent her youth and young adulthood in Milwaukee; emigrated to Palestine (now Israel) (1921); Israel's first woman Prime Minister (1969-74)

René Ménard (1605-1661), French Jesuit; first Roman Catholic priest known to be in Wisconsin

Alexander Mitchell (1817-1887), banker and political leader; owned interests in almost every railroad in Wisconsin, especially the Chicago, Milwaukee and St. Paul line; member of the United States House of Representatives (1871-75)

R.M. LA FOLLETTE, SR.

VINCE LOMBARDI

JOSEPH McCARTHY

GOLDA MEIR

BILLY MITCHELL

JOHN MUIR

GEORGIA O'KEEFFE

WILLIAM REHNQUIST

William L. (Billy) Mitchell (1879-1936), military leader and aviator; learned to fly from Orville Wright; pioneered military aviation (early 1900s); during World War I, organized and commanded United States air forces, in France; demoted and eventually court-martialed for criticizing military failure to develop air power; restored to army rolls as a major general (1942)

John Muir (1838-1914), born in Marquette County; naturalist and explorer; helped found Sierra Club; promoted development of national parks and forests

Jean Nicolet (1598-1642), French explorer; first European known to have seen Lake Michigan (1634); explored Green Bay, the Fox River, and most of the Wisconsin River.

Pat O'Brien (1899-1983), born in Milwaukee; actor; best known for role of Knute Rockne in film *Four Horsemen of the Apocalypse*

Albert Ochsner (1858-1925), born in Baraboo; physician; pioneered in treating cancer with radium

Georgia O'Keeffe (1887-1986), born in Sun Prairie; abstract painter; known for painting objects from nature in their simplest forms and colors

Oshkosh (1795-1858), Menominee Indian; fought in War of 1812; led the Menominee in a successful attempt to retain tribal lands in Wisconsin; as a result of his efforts the original Menominee reservation was granted by the federal government; city of Oshkosh is named for him

George Wilbur Peck (1840-1916), journalist and political leader; mayor of Milwaukee (1890); governor of Wisconsin (1891-95); author of "Peck's Bad Boy" stories about a mischievous boy

William Proxmire (1915-   ), political leader; United States senator (1957-   ); chairman of Senate Banking Committee (1975-81); noted for giving "Golden Fleece" awards to federal projects he considers wasteful

Pierre-Esprit, Sieur de Radisson (1636?-1710), French fur trader and explorer; with his brother-in-law Groseilliers, first European to identify Chequamegon Bay

William Hubbs Rehnquist (1924-   ), born in Milwaukee; jurist; associate justice of the United States Supreme Court (1971-86); chief justice (1986-   )

Ringling Brothers Albert (1852-1916), Otto (1858-1911), Alfred (1861-1919), Charles (1863-1926), John (1866-1936), born in Baraboo; circus promoters; operated a touring circus (1884); bought out rivals and established Ringling Brothers and Barnum and Bailey Circus (1919)

Jeremiah Rusk (1830-1893), political leader; governor of Wisconsin (1882-1889); first United States secretary of agriculture (1889)

Carl **Schurz** (1829-1906), lawyer, activist, author, political leader; edited German-language newspapers in Watertown; known for his passionate defense of antislavery causes; campaigned nationally for President Abraham Lincoln; Brigadier General in the Union Army during the Civil War; United States senator from Missouri; United States secretary of the interior

CARL SCHURZ

Margarethe Schurz (1833-1876), educator; opened first United States kindergarten, in Watertown (1856)

Donald K. (Deke) Slayton (1924-   ), born in Sparta; astronaut; aboard Project Mercury spaceflights (1962, 1963) and Apollo-Soyuz docking module (1975)

Walter Wellesley (Red) Smith (1905-1982), born in Green Bay; sportswriter; received 1976 Pulitzer Prize for newspaper writing; author of several books, including *Out of the Red* (1950) and *Press Box: Red Smith's Favorite Sports Stories* (1976)

James Jesse Strang (1813-1856), religious leader; after being expelled from his position as an elder of the Mormon Church (1844), led a colony of dissident Mormons in Walworth County (1844-47); moved to Beaver Island, Michigan (1847) and proclaimed himself "king"

SPENCER TRACY

Tommy G. Thompson (1941-   ), born in Elroy; lawyer and political leader; governor of Wisconsin (1987-   )

John Willard Toland (1912-   ), born in La Crosse; author, historian; books include *Adolf Hitler; The Last Hundred Days; But Not in Shame;* and *The Rising Sun: The Decline and Fall of the Japanese Empire, 1936-1945,* for which he received the 1971 Pulitzer Prize in non-fiction

Spencer Tracy (1900-1967), born in Milwaukee; actor; won Academy Awards as best actor in the films *Captains Courageous* (1937) and *Boys Town* (1938)

Daniel J. Travanti (1940-   ), born in Kenosha; actor; acting credits include starring role in television series "Hill Street Blues"

NATHAN TWINING

Nathan Farragut Twining (1897-1982), born in Monroe; United States Air Force general; led Air Force conversion to 100 percent jets; became chief of staff (1953); chairman of Joint Chiefs of Staff (1957-60)

Thorstein Bunde Veblen (1857-1929), born in Valders; economist and social scientist; attacked current economic theories in *The Theory of the Leisure Class* (1899)

William Freeman Vilas (1840-1908), lawyer, educator and political leader; postmaster general of the United States (1885-88); led development of the Rural Free Delivery system

(George) Orson Welles (1915-1985), born in Kenosha; actor and director; his radio drama *The War of the Worlds* (1938) was a terrifyingly realistic account of a Martian invasion; most famous of many films is *Citizen Kane* (1941)

ORSON WELLES

THORNTON WILDER

FRANK LLOYD WRIGHT

Gene Wilder (1935-), born in Milwaukee; actor; comedic film actor whose films include *The Producers* and *Young Frankenstein*

Laura Ingalls Wilder (1867-1957), born in Pepin; novelist; best known for *The Little House on the Prairie* (1935), an account of her childhood from which a long-running television series was adapted

Thornton Niven Wilder (1897-1975), born in Madison; novelist and dramatist; received Pulitzer Prizes for *The Bridge at San Luis Rey* (1928), *Our Town* (1938), and *The Skin of Our Teeth* (1943); awarded Presidential Medal of Freedom (1963) and the first National Medal for Literature (1965)

Frances Elizabeth Caroline Willard (1839-1898), social reformer; grew up near Janesville; organized Women's Christian Temperance Union (1874) and served as its president (1879-90); president of National Council of Women (1890)

Frank Lloyd Wright (1867-1959), born in Richland Center; architect; one of the United States' most influential architects; major Wisconsin buildings are S.C. Johnson & Son headquarters, Racine; First Unitarian Church, Madison; Taliesin, Spring Green (1911)

GOVERNORS

Nelson Dewey	1848-1852	John J. Blaine	1921-1927
Leonard J. Farwell	1852-1854	Fred R. Zimmerman	1927-1929
William A. Barstow	1854-1856	Walter J. Kohler, Sr.	1929-1931
Arthur McArthur	1856	Philip F. La Follette	1931-1933
Coles Bashford	1856-1858	Albert G. Schmedeman	1933-1935
Alexander W. Randall	1858-1862	Philip F. La Follette	1935-1939
Louis P. Harvey	1862	Julius P. Heil	1939-1943
Edward Salomon	1862-1864	Walter S. Goodland	1943-1947
James T. Lewis	1864-1866	Oscar Rennebohm	1947-1951
Lucius Fairchild	1866-1872	Walter J. Kohler, Jr.	1951-1957
Cadwallader C. Washburn	1872-1874	Vernon W. Thomson	1957-1959
William R. Taylor	1874-1876	Gaylord A. Nelson	1959-1963
Harrison Ludington	1876-1878	John W. Reynolds	1963-1965
William E. Smith	1878-1882	Warren P. Knowles	1965-1971
Jeremiah McLain Rusk	1882-1889	Patrick J. Lucey	1971-1977
William D. Hoard	1889-1891	Martin J. Schreiber	1977-1979
George W. Peck	1891-1895	Lee S. Dreyfus	1979-1983
William H. Upham	1895-1897	Anthony S. Earl	1983-1987
Edward Scofield	1897-1901	Tommy G. Thompson	1987-
Robert M. La Follette, Sr.	1901-1906		
James O. Davidson	1906-1911		
Francis E. McGovern	1911-1915		
Emanuel L. Philipp	1915-1921		

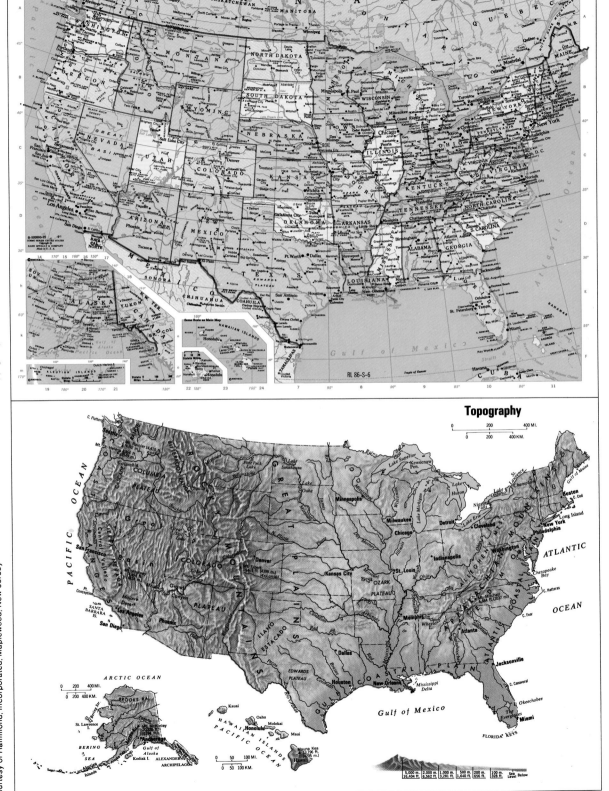

RL 86-S-6

Topography

MAP KEY

Longitude West of Greenwich

MINN.

Lake Superior

APOSTLE ISLANDS

MICH.

WIS.

MICH.

IOWA

ILLINOIS

Lake Michigan

Hibbing · Virginia · Biwabik · Mountain Iron · Buhl · Chisholm · Gilbert · Aurora · Eveleth

Two Harbors · Silver Bay · Beaver Bay · Bear I. · Outer I. · Oak I. · Stockton I. · Michigan I. · Fourteen Mile Pt.

Duluth · Superior · Proctor · Cloquet · Carlton · Oliver · Foxboro · Patzau · Bennett

Port Wing · Cornucopia · Bayfield · La Pointe · Washburn · Red Cliff · Ontonagon · White Pine

Ashland · Odanah · Saxon · Ramsay · Bessemer · Ironwood · Wakefield · Hurley · Montreal · Upson · Iron Belt · Mellen · Marengo · Gurney · Benoit · Mason · Sanborn · Grandview · Morse · Glidden · Presque Isle · Land O' Lakes

MT. WHITTLESEY 1872

Moose Lake · Solon Springs · Dairyland · Gordon · Cable · Namekagon · Drummond

Sandstone · Danbury · Webster · Spooner · Siren · Grantsburg · Lewis · Frederic · Trego · Stone Lake · Springbrook · Hayward · Minong · Couderay · Reserve · Loretta · Fifield · Park Falls · Winter · Radisson · Phillips · Woodboro · Rhinelander · Mercer · Butternut · Sayner · Phelps · Iron River · Stambaugh · Caspian

Luck · Milltown · Centuria · Osceola · Dresser · St. Croix Falls · Clayton · Amery · Clear Lake · Cumberland · Rice Lake · Birchwood · Haugen · Almena · Mikana · Exeland · Ladysmith · Ingram · Kennan · Calawba · Hawkins · Tripoli · Heafford Junction · Tomahawk · Crandon · Cavour · Goodman · Dunbar · Pembine · Niagara · Norway · Vulcan · Iron Mountain · Spread Eagle · Long Lake · Kingsford · Aurora · Florence · Fence · Gladstone · Escanaba · Hermansville

Cameron · Barronett · Turtle Lake · Comstock · Canton · Bruce · Conrath · Sheldon · Westboro · Ogema · Rib Lake · Prentice · TIMMS HILL 1952 HIGHEST IN WIS. · Chelsea · Merrill · Gleason · Bryant · Elton · Antigo · Polar · White Lake · Mountain · Beaver · Pound · Coleman · Suring · Lena · Pensaukee · Oconto · Abrams · Sturgeon Bay · Menominee · Marinette · Peshtigo · Egg Harbor · Baileys Harbor · Cave Point

Star Prairie · New Richmond · Somerset · Stillwater · Roberts · Hammond · Hudson · Baldwin · Woodville · Glenwood City · Boyceville · Downing · Knapp · Menomonie · Elk Mound · Colfax · Wheeler · Sand Creek · Bloomer · Chippewa Falls · Eau Claire · Altoona · Eau Claire · Jim Falls · Cadott · Stanley · Thorp · Withee · Curtiss · Abbotsford · Colby · Dorchester · Stetsonville · Medford · Gilman · Lublin · Athens · Marathon · Edgar · Wausau · Schofield · Hatley · Rothschild · Mosinee · Eland · Bowler · Gresham · Shawano · Cecil · Green Valley · Navarino · Pulaski · Little Suamico · Brussels · Forestville · Dyckesville · Casco · Luxemburg · Algoma

RIB MTN. 1940

Hastings · Prescott · River Falls · Ellsworth · Diamond Bluff · Bay City · Maiden Rock · Spring Valley · Martell · Elmwood · Rock Elm · Arkansaw · Durand · Eau Galle · Foster · Eleva · Augusta · Fairchild · Osseo · Strum · Willard · Greenwood · Loyal · Stratford · Spencer · Marshfield · Auburndale · Chili · Hewitt · Granton · Neillsville · Milladore · Junction City · Vesper · Arpin · Stevens Point · Rosholt · Iola · Scandinavia · Amherst · Plover · Manawa · Clintonville · Bear Creek · Seymour · Howard · New Franken · Kewaunee

Red Wing · Stockholm · Pepin · Arcadia · Cochrane · Mondovi · Gilmanton · Modena · Northfield · Pigeon Falls · Whitehall · Independence · Ettrick · Blair · Taylor · Hixton · Black River Falls · Pleasant View · Merrillan · Humbird · Pittsville · Wisconsin Rapids · Babcock · Nekoosa · Port Edwards · Biron · Whiting · Plainfield · Hancock · Wild Rose · Poy Sippi · Weyauwega · Fremont · Waupaca · King · Almond · Bancroft · Royalton · New London · Hortonville · Black Creek · Shiocton · Appleton · Kaukauna · Little Chute · Menasha · Neenah · De Pere · Green Bay · Wrightstown · Denmark · Stangelville · Mishicot · Two Rivers · Manitowoc

Wabasha · Lake City · Alma · Buffalo City · Fountain City · Cataract · Tomah · Warrens · Wyeville · Necedah · Mather · Camp Douglas · Friendship · Adams · Wautoma · Redgranite · Berlin · Omro · Oshkosh · Winneconne · Eureka · Waukau · Ripon · Brandon · Green Lake · N. Fond du Lac · Rosendale · Fairwater · Fond du Lac · Eden · Campbellsport · Kewaskum · West Bend · Newburg · Fredonia · Belgium · Port Washington · Kohler · Sheboygan · Sheboygan Falls · Plymouth · Oostburg · Cedar Grove · Random Lake · Adell · Cascade · Glenbeulah · Kiel · New Holstein · Elkhart Lake · St. Cloud · Calvary · Mt. Calvary · Marytown · Johnsburg · Charlesburg · Brothertown · New Holstein

Rochester · Winona · Trempealeau · Galesville · Holmen · Onalaska · La Crosse · W. Salem · Bangor · Sparta · Norwalk · Wilton · Kendall · Ontario · Hillsboro · Elroy · Union Center · Wonewoc · Mauston · New Lisbon · Lyndon Station · Grand Marsh · Westfield · Neshkoro · Montello · Packwaukee · Endeavor · Briggsville · Oxford · Markesan

Zumbrota · Pine Island · Plainview · Altura · Dodge · North Bend · Melrose · Cashton · Cheseburg · Westby · Coon Valley · Stoddard · Genoa · Viroqua · Victory · De Soto · Readstown · La Farge · Soldiers Grove · Gays Mills · Seneca · Mt. Sterling · Steuben · Boscobel · Wauzeka · Eastman · Prairie du Chien · Lynxville · Ferryville · Gotham · Richland Center · Loganville · Rock Springs · Cazenovia · La Valle · Reedsburg · Baraboo · THE DELLS · Wisconsin Dells · Portage · Cambria · Pardeeville · Rio · Poynette · Fall River · Lowell · Columbus · Randolph · Fox Lake · Beaver Dam · Juneau · Horicon · Mayville · Theresa · Lomira · Allenton · Hartford · Neosho · Slinger · Richfield · Germantown · Menomonee Falls · Cedarburg · Grafton · Thiensville · Mequon · Saukville

St. Charles · St. Francis · Mineral Point · Dodgeville · Ridgeway · Barneveld · Blue River · Avoca · Lone Rock · Spring Green · Arena · Mazomanie · Cross Plains · Middleton · Madison · Monona · Sun Prairie · Waunakee · De Forest · Deerfield · Marshall · Cottage Grove · Cambridge · Stoughton · Jefferson · Ft. Atkinson · Palmyra · Eagle · Mukwonago · Waukesha · Pewaukee · Hartland · Delafield · Dousman · New Berlin · Brookfield · Wauwatosa · Milwaukee · West Allis · Greenfield · Cudahy · S. Milwaukee · Oak Creek · Franklin · Greendale

Dubuque · East Dubuque · Galena · Cassville · Potosi · Platteville · Hazel Green · Benton · Shullsburg · Cuba City · Dickeyville · Belmont · Lancaster · Montfort · Livingston · Highland · Cobb · Fennimore · Bloomington · Boscobel · Darlington · Gratiot · S. Wayne · Browntown · Juda · Monroe · Orfordville · Argyle · Blanchardville · Hollandale · Belleville · New Glarus · Monticello · Albany · Footville · Evansville · Brooklyn · Oregon · Verona · Edgerton · Milton · Janesville · Whitewater · Palmyra · Elkhorn · Delavan · Darien · Williams Bay · Lake Geneva · Genoa City · Fontana · Sharon · Walworth · Silver Lake · Twin Lakes · Antioch · Zion · Waukegan · Beloit · Rockton · Harvard · Woodstock · Fox Lake · McHenry · Grayslake · Libertyville · Lake Forest · Mundelein · Highland Park · Barrington · Glencoe · Winnetka · Wilmette · Palatine · Arlington Hts.

Warren · Dyersville · Cascade · Bellevue · 52055012 CONDE SERIES WISCONSIN RAND MCNALLY & COMPANY Made in U.S.A. · Stockton · Lena · Freeport · Pecatonica · Rockford · Belvidere · Marengo · Crystal Lake · Genoa City · N. Chicago

Mount Carroll · Lanark · Forreston · Byron · Savanna

Inset: Green Bay area

Green Bay · De Pere · Allouez · Ashwaubenon · Seymour · Oneida · Howard · New Franken · Pilsen · Shiocton · Black Creek · Freedom · Wrightstown · Greenleaf · Cooperstown · Denmark · Stangelville · Tisch Mills · Appleton · Mackville · Greenville · Little Chute · Kaukauna · Combined Locks · Kimberly · Morrison · Maribel · Wayside · Francis Creek · Kellnersville · Menasha · Neenah · Forest Junction · Reedsville · Branch · Two Rivers · Sherwood · Hilbert · Brillion · Potter · Whitelaw · Manitowoc · Winnebago · Stockbridge · Collins · Gravesville · Valders · St. Nazianz · Oshkosh · Chilton · Hayton · Cleveland · Brothertown · New Holstein · Charlesburg · Newton · Calumetville · Pipe · Marytown · Johnsburg · St. Anna · Kiel · Elkhart Lake · Howards Grove · Haven · N. Fond du Lac · Vandyne · Peebles · Mount Calvary · Calvary · Taycheedah · Glenbeulah · Greenbush · Fond du Lac · Kohler · Sheboygan

Inset: Milwaukee area

Milwaukee · Wauwatosa · W. Allis · W. Milwaukee · St. Francis · Cudahy · S. Milwaukee · Slinger · Jackson · Grafton · Cedarburg · Hartford · Rockfield · Thiensville · Mequon · Richfield · Germantown · Brown Deer · Bayside · Menomonee Falls · N. Lake · Merton · Lannon · River Hills · Fox Point · Chenequa · Sussex · Butler · Whitefish Bay · Hartland · Pewaukee · Brookfield · Shorewood · Delafield · Elm Grove · Waukesha · Genesee Depot · New Berlin · Greenfield · Waubesa · Muskego · Hales Corners · Greendale · Big Bend · Mukwonago · Oak Creek · Franklin · Lake Beulah · Wind Lake · Waterford · Rochester · Honey Creek · N. Cape · Franksville · Wind Point · Kansasville · Burlington · Sturtevant · Racine · Union Grove · Somers · Lyons · Kenosha · New Munster · Silver Lake · Paddock Lake · Salem · Bristol · Pleasant Prairie · Pell Lake · Bassett · Genoa City · Twin Lakes · Trevor · Winthrop Harbor · Antioch

Statute Miles 5 0 5 10 20 30 40
Kilometers 5 0 5 15 25 35 45 55

Lambert Conformal Conic Projection

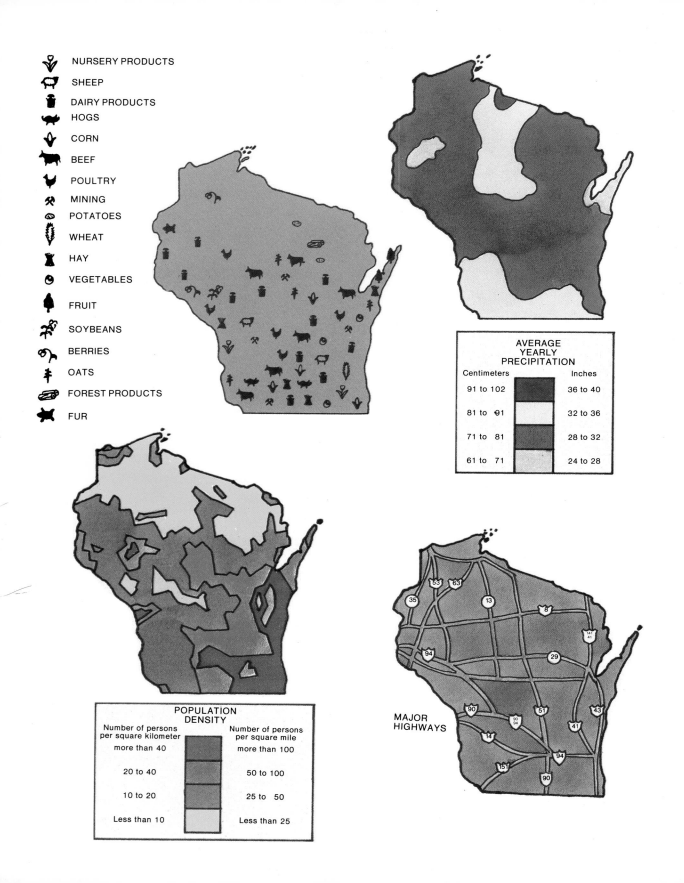

NURSERY PRODUCTS
SHEEP
DAIRY PRODUCTS
HOGS
CORN
BEEF
POULTRY
MINING
POTATOES
WHEAT
HAY
VEGETABLES
FRUIT
SOYBEANS
BERRIES
OATS
FOREST PRODUCTS
FUR

AVERAGE YEARLY PRECIPITATION

Centimeters		Inches
91 to 102		36 to 40
81 to 91		32 to 36
71 to 81		28 to 32
61 to 71		24 to 28

POPULATION DENSITY

Number of persons per square kilometer		Number of persons per square mile
more than 40		more than 100
20 to 40		50 to 100
10 to 20		25 to 50
Less than 10		Less than 25

MAJOR HIGHWAYS

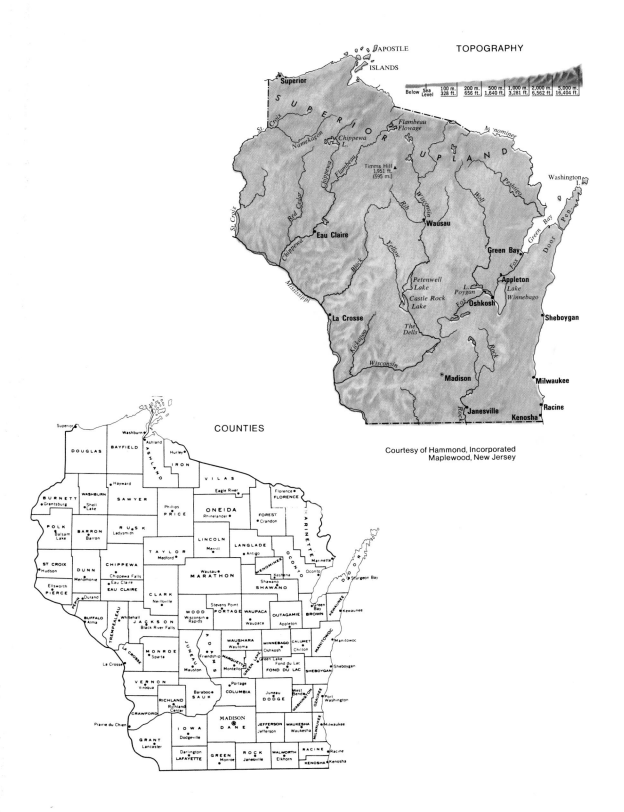

TOPOGRAPHY

Below Sea Level | 100 m. 328 ft. | 200 m. 656 ft. | 500 m. 1,640 ft. | 1,000 m. 3,281 ft. | 2,000 m. 6,562 ft. | 5,000 m. 16,404 ft.

APOSTLE ISLANDS

Superior

SUPERIOR

St. Croix
Namekagon
Chippewa L.
Flambeau Flowage

Menominee

Washington I.

U P L A N D

Timms Hill 1,951 ft. (595 m.)

Red Cedar
Chippewa
Flambeau
Rib
Wisconsin
Wolf
Peshtigo

Green Bay

Wausau

Eau Claire

Chippewa
Yellow
Black

Green Bay

Door Pen.

Petenwell Lake
Castle Rock Lake

Fox
L. Poygan
Appleton
Lake Winnebago

Oshkosh

Mississippi

La Crosse

Sheboygan

Kickapoo

The Dells

Rock

Wisconsin

Madison

Milwaukee

Janesville

Racine

Kenosha

COUNTIES

Courtesy of Hammond, Incorporated
Maplewood, New Jersey

Superior

DOUGLAS
BAYFIELD
Washburn
Ashland
ASHLAND
Hurley
IRON
VILAS

Hayward
Eagle River
Florence
FLORENCE

BURNETT
WASHBURN
Shell Lake
SAWYER
Phillips
PRICE
ONEIDA
Rhinelander
FOREST
Crandon

Grantsburg

POLK
Balsam Lake
BARRON
Barron
RUSK
Ladysmith
LINCOLN
Merrill
LANGLADE
Antigo
MARINETTE
Marinette

ST CROIX
Hudson
DUNN
Menomonie
CHIPPEWA
Chippewa Falls
TAYLOR
Medford
MARATHON
Wausau
MENOMINEE
Keshena
Shawano
SHAWANO
OCONTO
Oconto
DOOR
Sturgeon Bay

Ellsworth
PIERCE
Durand
Eau Claire
EAU CLAIRE
CLARK
Neillsville

BUFFALO
Alma
TREMPEALEAU
Whitehall
JACKSON
Black River Falls
WOOD
Wisconsin Rapids
PORTAGE
Stevens Point
WAUPACA
Waupaca
OUTAGAMIE
Appleton
BROWN
Green Bay
KEWAUNEE
Kewaunee

LA CROSSE
La Crosse
MONROE
Sparta
JUNEAU
Friendship
WAUSHARA
Wautoma
WINNEBAGO
Oshkosh
CALUMET
Chilton
MANITOWOC
Manitowoc

VERNON
Viroqua
Mauston
Montello
MARQUETTE
GREEN LAKE
Green Lake
FOND DU LAC
Fond du Lac
SHEBOYGAN
Sheboygan

RICHLAND
Richland Center
SAUK
Baraboo
COLUMBIA
Portage
Juneau
DODGE
West Bend
WASHINGTON
Port Washington
OZAUKEE

CRAWFORD
Prairie du Chien
IOWA
Dodgeville
DANE
MADISON
JEFFERSON
Jefferson
WAUKESHA
Waukesha
MILWAUKEE
Milwaukee

GRANT
Lancaster
LAFAYETTE
Darlington
GREEN
Monroe
ROCK
Janesville
WALWORTH
Elkhorn
RACINE
Racine
KENOSHA
Kenosha

Dells Mill, in Augusta

INDEX

Page numbers that appear in boldface type indicate illustrations

138

During the warm months of the year, students at the University of Wisconsin gather on the terrace of the Student Union to eat lunch, study, read, chat, or just enjoy the view of beautiful Lake Mendota.

Picture Identifications

Front cover: Wisconsin dairy farm
Back cover: Milwaukee lakefront
Pages 2-3: Stonefield Village and the Mississippi River
Page 6: Sugar maples near the Wolf River, Menominee Indian Reservation
Pages 8-9: Fertile farmland near Holmen in LaCrosse County
Pages 20-21: Montage of Wisconsin residents
Page 27: A historical reenactment of Father Jacques Marquette's voyage of exploration
Pages 38-39: Old World Wisconsin
Page 54: Milwaukee as it looked in 1873
Page 70: The State Capitol in Madison
Pages 80-81: Children on the rocks at the dells of the Eau Claire River in Marathon County
Page 80 (inset): Elkhart Lake auto race
Pages 94-95: Gills Rock, Door County
Page 94 (inset): Aerial view of the Milwaukee lakefront at night
Page 108: Montage showing the state flag, the state bird (robin), the state tree (sugar maple), the state flower (wood violet), the state animal (badger), and the state mineral (Galena)

About the Author

R. Conrad Stein was born and grew up in Chicago. He began writing professionally shortly after graduating from the University of Illinois. He is the author of many books, articles, and short stories written for young readers. As a lifelong resident of neighboring Illinois, Mr. Stein has been visiting Wisconsin since he was a boy. To prepare for this book, he drove through Wisconsin's cities, forests, and farmlands, stopping often to chat with the people. He found Wisconsinites to be frank, friendly, and immensely proud of their state.

Picture Acknowledgments

H. Armstrong Roberts: Pages 41, 99 (right), 113, 122 (right), 131 (Schurz); © B. Vogel: Front cover; © H. Abernathy: Pages 2-3; © T. Algire: Pages 12 (left), 79; © K. Vreeland: Pages 94-95; © Roger A. Lloyd: Page 141
© **Tim Downing:** Page 4
Third Coast: © Alan Magayne-Roshak: Back Cover, page 102; © Ken Dequaine: Pages 5, 8-9, 12 (right), 76 (right), 114 (right); © Letty Stasko: Page 15 (top); © William Meyer: Pages 21 (top right and bottom left), 63, 90 (left), 119 (right); © Paul H. Henning: Pages 21 (top left), 73; © Robert E. Gantner: Page 29 (left); © Phil Moughmer: Page 50; © Brent Nicastro: Pages 70, 74 (right), 100; © Ralf-Finn Hestoft: Page 74 (left); © William L. Stonecipher: Pages 80-81; © R. Bublitz: Page 85; © E.J. Purcell: Page 86 (right); © Betty Fernald-Maier: Page 90 (right); © Jeff Lowe: Page 92 (left); © Alan Jung: Page 92 (right); © Scott Housom: Page 94 (inset); © Sue Hagan: Page 105; © Bruce Brander: Page 119 (left); © Robert D. Schaap: Page 138
© **Lynn M. Stone:** Pages 6, 15 (bottom), 108 (background and bottom left)
Tom Stack & Associates: © Tom Algire: Page 11
Nawrocki Stock Photo: © Will Fields: Page 12 (middle); © David Lissy: Page 21 (middle right and bottom right); © T.J. Florian: Page 25; © Robert Lightfoot: Page 27; © D.J. Variakojis: Pages 38-39
© **James P. Rowan:** Pages 16, 89, 97 (left), 99 (left), 106
© **Jerry Hennen:** Page 19
© **Martin Hintz:** Page 20 (top left, top right, bottom left)
R/C Photo Agency: © Richard L. Capps: Page 20 (bottom right); © J.M. Halama: Page 78; © Betty A. Kubis: Page 80 (inset); © J. Madeley: Page 97 (right)
© **Cameramann International Ltd.:** Pages 20 (middle left), 76 (left), 86 (left), 98
Odyssey Productions: © Robert Frerck: Page 21 (middle left)
Wide World Photos: Pages 24, 61 (bottom), 67 (left), 126 (Abrahamson), 127 (Groppi), 128 (Kennan), 131 (Twining)
© **Reinhard Brucker:** Pages 29 (right), 108 (bottom right), 122 (left)
Historical Pictures Service, Inc., Chicago: Pages 31, 33, 34, 37, 44, 46, 52, 54, 61 (top left), 132 (Wright)
Photri: Page 131 (Welles); © Dorothy Steinle: Page 114 (left); © Dr. C.W. Biedel: Page 104
The Bettmann Archive: Pages 49 (right and bottom left), 57, 58, 61 (right), 83, 127 (Ferber and Herman), 128 (Houdini and Kaltenborn), 129 (LaFollette), 130 (Mitchell and Muir), 131 (Tracy), 132 (Wilder)
UPI/Bettmann: Pages 65, 67 (right), 126 (Bardeen), 127 (Gesell), 128 (Hirsch), 129 (Lombardi, McCarthy, and Meir), 130 (O'Keeffe and Rehnquist)
© **Virginia Grimes:** Page 51
© **Art Pahlke:** Page 68
Frank Lloyd Wright Foundation: Page 85 (left)
Joan Dunlop: Page 88
Root Resources: © Mary and Loren Root: Page 108 (top left); © Sherrill Lynch: Page 108 (top right)
Marilyn Gartman Agency: © Michael Philip Manheim: Page 110
© **Chandler Forman:** Page 121
Len W. Meents: Maps on pages 98, 100, 102, 105, 136
Courtesy Flag Research Center, Winchester, Massachusetts 01890: Flag on page 108